THIS
INDIAN
KID

A NATIVE AMERICAN MEMOIR

Praise for
THIS INDIAN KID
by EDDIE CHUCULATE

"A tightly crafted story about coming of age in Oklahoma from Eddie Chuculate, a writer of breathtaking lyricism and remarkable candor. *This Indian Kid* is nostalgia at its most potent." —Luke Jerod Kummer, author of *The Blue Period: A Novel* and *Takers Mad*

"Chuculate's memoir is a story of tremendous strength, courage, and resilience, with a message of hope. Here we witness Native American life in the heartland of America with a critical eye toward racism, poverty, and bullying, and skillfully executed with heart and compassion. I highly recommend THIS INDIAN KID, because I found myself absorbed by its genuine rendition of Oklahoma, of Native diversity, and of the complexities of the human experience." —Oscar Hokeah, author of *Calling for a Blanket Dance*

"Anyone who's grown up in America will find Eddie Chuculate's *This Indian Kid* to be as satisfying as a cold drink of water on a blazing hot day. With his razor-sharp eye for detail, Chuculate reveals the heartache and joy of everyday life. This is a remarkable book that will stick with you long after you're finished." —Rus Bradburd, author of *All the Dreams We've Dreamed: A Story of Hoops* and *Handguns on Chicago's West Side*

ALSO BY EDDIE CHUCULATE

CHEYENNE MADONNA

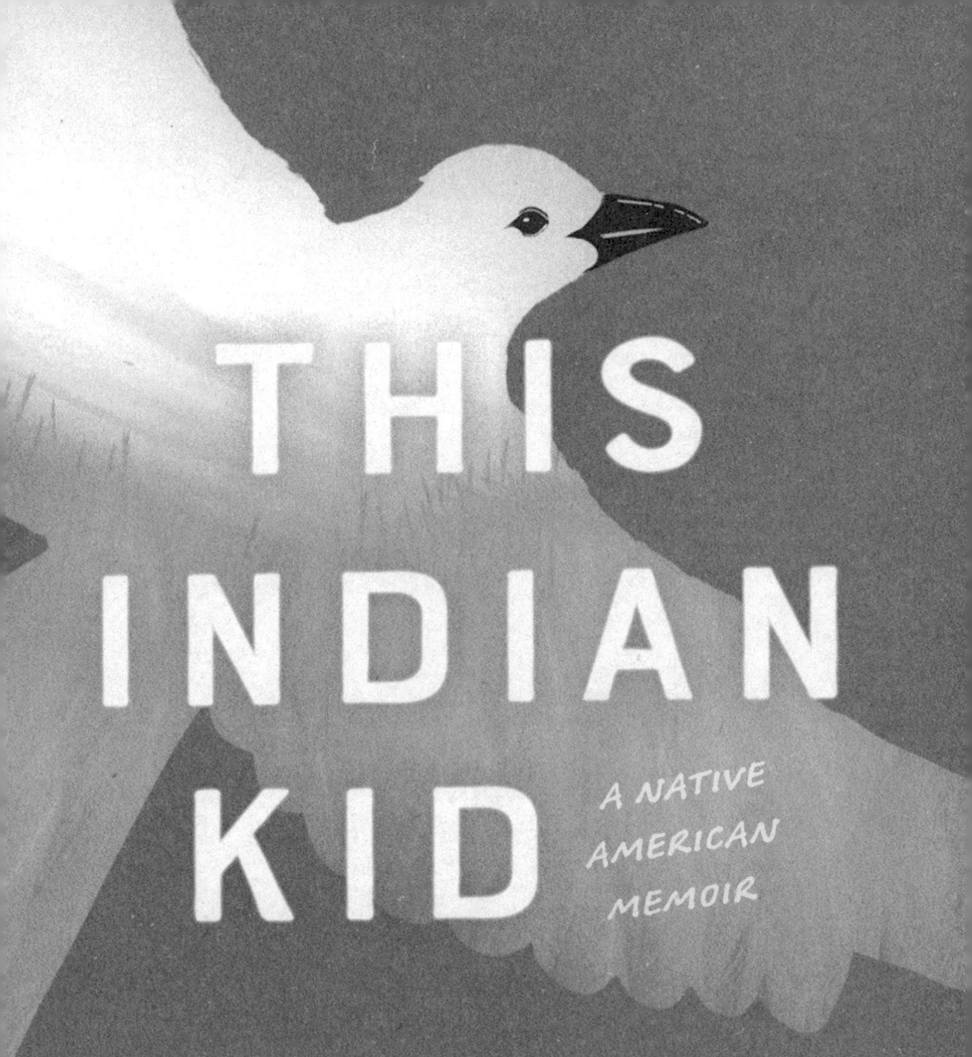

THIS INDIAN KID

A NATIVE AMERICAN MEMOIR

EDDIE CHUCULATE

SCHOLASTIC
FOCUS

Library of Congress Cataloging-in-Publication Data

Names: Chuculate, Eddie D., author.
Title: This Indian kid : a Native American memoir / Eddie Chuculate.
Other titles: Native American memoir
Description: First edition. | New York, NY : Scholastic Focus, 2023. | Audience: Ages 12 and up | Audience: Grades 10–12 | Summary: "Award-winning author Eddie Chuculate recounts his experience growing up in rural Oklahoma, from boyhood to young manhood, in an evocative and vivid voice. "Granny was full-blood Creek, but the Bureau of Indian Affairs insisted she was thirteen-sixteenths. She showed her card to me. I'd sit at the kitchen table and stare at her when she was eating, wondering how you could be thirteen-sixteenths of anything and if so, what part of her constituted the other three-sixteenths." Growing up impoverished and shuttled between different households, it seemed life was bound to take a certain path for Eddie Chuculate. Despite the challenges he faced, his upbringing was rich with love and bountiful lessons from his Creek and Cherokee heritage, deep-rooted traditions he embraced even as he learned to live within the culture of white, small-town America that dominated his migratory childhood. Award-winning author Eddie Chuculate brings his childhood to life with spare, unflinching prose. This book is at once a love letter to his Native American roots and an inspiring and essential message for young readers everywhere, who are coming of age in an era when conversations about acceptance and empathy, love and perspective are more necessary than ever before. "— Provided by publisher.
Identifiers: LCCN 2023005172 | ISBN 9781338802085 (hardcover) | ISBN 9781338802108 (ebook)
Subjects: LCSH: Chuculate, Eddie D.—Childhood and youth—Juvenile literature. | Creek Indians—Oklahoma—Muskogee—Biography—Juvenile literature. | Cherokee Indians—Oklahoma—Muskogee—Biography—Juvenile literature. | Muskogee (Okla.)—Social life and customs—20th century—Juvenile literature. | Muskogee (Okla.)—Race relations—History—20th century—Juvenile literature. | Muskogee (Okla.)—Biography—Juvenile literature.
Classification: LCC E99.C9 C48 2023 | DDC 976.6004/97385092 [B]—dc23/eng/20230221
LC record available at https://lccn.loc.gov/2023005172

10 9 8 7 6 5 4 3 2 1   23 24 25 26 27

Printed in the U.S.A.   37

First edition, September 2023

Book design by Cassy Price
Map on pages xii-xiii by Jim McMahon

To Momma

THIS
INDIAN
KID

A NATIVE AMERICAN MEMOIR

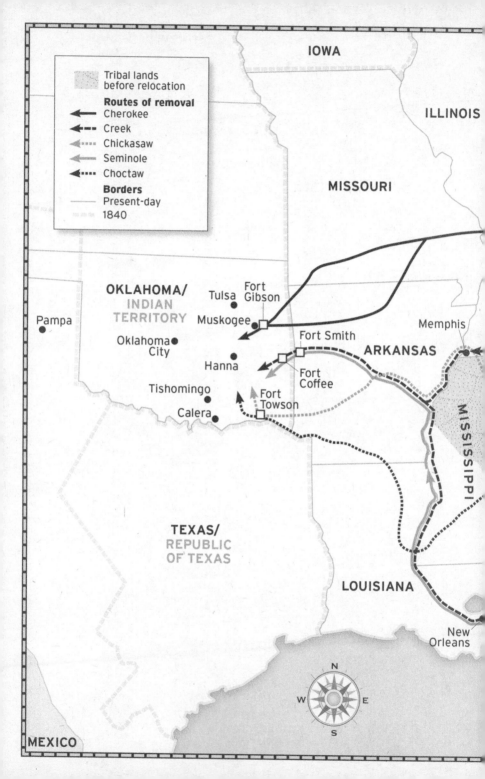

PENNSYLVANIA

MARYLAND

OHIO

INDIANA

WEST
VIRGINIA

VIRGINIA

KENTUCKY

NORTH
CAROLINA

TENNESSEE

SOUTH
CAROLINA

GEORGIA

ALABAMA

Fort
Mitchell

ATLANTIC
OCEAN

FORIDA/
FLORIDA
TERRITORY

Gulf of Mexico

| 0 | | 100 MI |

| 0 | | 100 KM |

A NOTE FROM THE AUTHOR

Following the adage about writing what you'd like to read, I realized I hadn't read much about growing up Native in the 1970s and '80s—snippets from a larger work, maybe, but not set exclusively in that era. And to be even more specific, about growing up in Oklahoma. I felt compelled to write an account of my childhood living in cities and towns among mixed races (although still primarily white), religions, and lifestyles.

I think you'll identify with characters in everyday circumstances similar to your own, providing a realistic lens to observe aspects of modern Native life. Native life certainly can be foreign to the non-Native and seem fantastic and supernatural, but more often it's an everyday life of going to school or work, playing sports, enjoying the outdoors, celebrating and mourning with friends and family.

I also hope you'll realize you can overcome mistakes—rise above them—and not be defined by your circumstances. You'll encounter racism along the way, but don't allow yourself to conform to outdated beliefs and attitudes of others—whether it be from peers or older generations. Know that it's good to be proud of your race, but realize other races will play big roles in your life as well.

I sincerely hope you enjoy reading the story from *This Indian Kid*. Let me know.

Sincerely,

Eddie Chuculate

First-grade photo at Calera (OK) Elementary in 1972–73. I was there long enough to have my picture taken in my giraffe shirt before transferring to Irving Elementary in Muskogee, Oklahoma. (Courtesy of the author.)

PROLOGUE

WETUMKA, WAURIKA, WAPANUCKA, Weleetka: Names on the map sing like poetry. Coweta, Chickasha, Tecumseh, Pawhuska: words rooted in Indigenous mother tongues invading English. Skiatook, Talihina, Washita, Oologah: Where are they who named you? Tuskahoma, Watonga, Anadarko, Bokchito: They roll off the tongue and echo across Oklahoma.

Oklahoma—with thirty-nine tribal nations and half a million people of Native ancestry—is Indian land. Even the name is derived from Choctaw words roughly translating to "red people." Your state or town quite likely originates from a Native American word, too.

The land was acquired by treaties with the US government and acts of Congress and called Indian Territory before it became Oklahoma. It comprises not only lakes, rivers, woods, and prairie, but cities, counties, and towns. Farms and ranches occupy Indian land along with factories, skyscrapers, and shopping malls. Public schools in Oklahoma have students of many races.

My maternal great-great-grandfather was a full-blood Creek named Jackson Lewis. His parents came to Indian Territory from their homeland in Alabama after being herded out with 20,000 others at gunpoint and bayonet by the United States military in the forced removal known romantically as the Trail of Tears. After walking 400 miles, more than 300 Creeks drowned when the steamboat they were packed onto struck another boat in the Mississippi River near Baton Rouge, a few hours after leaving New Orleans, in October 1837.

But that was just one segment of several journeys on wagons, afoot, and on horseback; in bitter winter conditions, the southeastern tribes endured. Tens of thousands died either during the exodus or after arrival. If they managed to stay alive, they were awarded 160 acres of land in Indian Territory. After Jackson's parents left Alabama in 1834, I was born at Claremore (OK) Indian Hospital five generations later.

My dad's father was Edward Chuculate—my namesake, although Eddie appears on my birth certificate—a full-blood Cherokee whose grandparents were forced from their homes in North Carolina as kids and orphaned on the removal on a northern route that trapped hundreds for weeks alongside the frozen Mississippi River. In Oklahoma, Ed married Martha Lundbeck, a Norwegian American missionary from North Dakota. So I'm part Norwegian but never really claimed it. Both of my grandfathers were full-blood Indian Baptist preachers who delivered sermons in their Native languages and in English. My dad also spoke both.

We're issued cards by the federal government stating what percentage of Indian blood we are. Growing up, I was shuttled between my mom and her mother, Maxine Mae (Narcomey) Flanary, who, thanks to me, became a grandmother at age thirty-six. Granny was full-blood Creek, but the Bureau of Indian Affairs insisted she was thirteen-sixteenths. She showed her card to me. I'd sit at the kitchen table and stare at her when she was eating, wondering how you could be a thirteen-sixteenths of anything and if so, what part of her constituted the other three-sixteenths. I determined it must be the three strands of white hair wisping from her brown forehead.

CHAPTER 1

MONKEY TAIL AND Cookie chased the rabbit around the bank of the frozen pond, their bark-howl filling the universe. When the rabbit turned the corner in a gallop like a racehorse, sun broke from the clouds, sparkling the snow like sugar, and we had to shield our eyes.

"They're running him right at us," my best friend and baseball teammate Lonnie Hill said, and I saw the pride in his eyes. I was in sixth grade in Muskogee, Lonnie in fifth but only two months younger, both of us out on Christmas vacation.

Lonnie raised his arm for me to stop and cautiously leveled his shotgun at the solitary rabbit, gray against the snow-white landscape, now standing on its hind legs, sniffing the air. The red lights of the KMUS radio towers blinked in the distance.

"Tell your Granny to get her skillet ready," Lonnie said out of the side of his mouth, cheek flattened against the stock. "This one's dead meat." His breath puffed the air like steam. He shucked a shell into the chamber; the clack rattled the silence.

I knelt and watched, knee crunching snow.

The cottontail scooted ahead a few yards, nose to the ground. Lonnie lowered the barrel momentarily, then raised it again. The blast exploded clods of black dirt right behind the rabbit, which

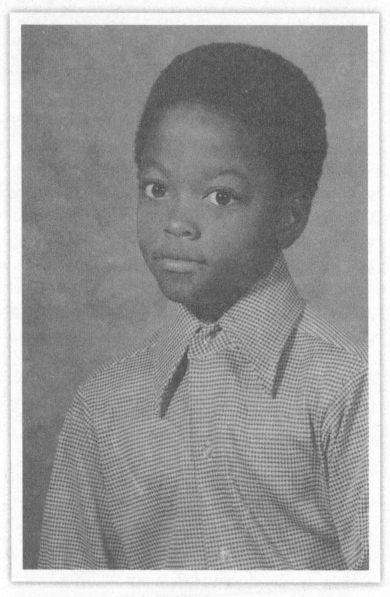

Lonnie Ray Hill, Jr., age eleven, 1976–77, Muskogee. Lonnie routinely walked about half a mile up a gravel road to see me, carrying either a fishing rod, shotgun, or baseball bat, his beagle dogs trailing him. (Courtesy of Melita Griffith.)

cartwheeled. His second shot sprayed a fountain of snow just in front of it. The rabbit reversed and darted straight for the pond, Monkey Tail and Cookie yowling right behind its flashing white tail. The shots echoed over the pastures.

"C'moan," Lonnie said, "they're on him now!"

I took off after Lonnie with my BB gun, stumbling over skeletons of brown brush that poked through the snow. The rabbit veered and slashed, always toward the pond, an oval rink dusted with snow. The barking beagle pups tangled and fell trying to copy the rabbit's moves, but they scrambled up howling and resumed pursuit.

The sun dipped into the clouds again and it grew dim. A shadow slid across the pond as the rabbit sprang from the bank, hit the ice, and went spinning like Bambi in a Disney cartoon. Lonnie aimed and pulled the trigger but the gun clicked. As he fed another shell into it the rabbit regained its footing and shot across the surface, kicking up puffs of snow as it leaped onto the far rim and vanished in a blur into the bushes.

Monkey Tail stopped at the edge of the pond, but Cookie jumped onto the ice, tumbled, and I heard a grumble in her throat. Cookie tried to walk but slipped onto her chest each time. She finally gave up in the middle of the pond and froze, looking all around.

"Cookie!" Lonnie yelled. "Come here, girl."

The dog looked up at Lonnie, whimpering.

"Come here, girl!" Lonnie whistled and smacked his thigh. "C'moan now."

Cookie barked at him, then panted, her tongue hanging like

a piece of bubblegum. She sat on her hind legs, whimpered, and barked at Lonnie. Monkey Tail joined us. He barked at Cookie, too.

Lonnie's uncle had given the pups to him last year. He'd brought them over to show me the day after, walking them down the dirt road. He'd seemed as happy as if he'd been given a stack of money.

"Dang it," he said. "Here, hold this."

Lonnie broke the gun open and handed it to me. I was astounded at its weight compared to my BB gun. I wasn't much of a hunter, only plunked at aluminum cans, birds, or turtles in the pond. Granny only let me go hunting with Lonnie because she trusted him. He knew all the regulations, wore a blaze-orange hunting vest, and kept the gun on safety and angled to the ground.

Lonnie tested the edge with his foot, stomped on it, then crept on.

"Come here, Cookie," he said in a soft voice, and whistled.

Cookie just whined and barked and would not move.

Lonnie eased out toward the middle, testing the surface every few feet with his boot. Cookie barked and wagged her rump as Lonnie inched closer. As he knelt to pick her up, the ice cracked and spider-webbed in long veins. He plunged in over his head with an arm stretched to the sky and Cookie went under, too.

"Lonnie!" I yelled.

He submerged for an instant and came back up, pawing at a big plate of ice, spewing water and yelling. He got a knee up onto a jagged shelf, then it broke off with a big crunch, and he fell in again on his back, disappearing. He resurfaced dog-paddling, thrashing and kicking, chopping and splashing water.

I ran around to the opposite bank, tripping and falling in snow with Monkey Tail barking at my heels. Lonnie had his head above water, elbows resting on a sheet of ice. It was thicker near the bank, so I inched out on my belly with the BB gun extended. He grabbed the barrel, and with both of us pulling like a tug-of-war, he slid onto the thicker section and stood up.

My small house was visible to the northwest, smoke trailing a thin line from the chimney, firewood stacked high out front. We jogged toward it, high-stepping and stomping through the snow, and as we neared I saw the windows fogged with steam at the corners. Dripping icicles hung from the porch roof like a row of fangs, but inside it looked warm and inviting.

We banged in.

"Granny!" I yelled, "Lonnie fell into the pond and lost his dog and gun and everything!"

"Oh, my word!" she said at the kitchen table where she sat with my great-uncle Chester.

Lonnie and I shivered and hopped with our arms crossed by the King woodstove, glowing red at the sides. It heated the whole house. Lonnie pawed pellets of ice from his hair onto the stove, where they puddled and steamed.

My grandpa Homer sat with his legs crossed in his chair across from us, holding the *Muskogee Daily Phoenix* spread open wide before him. It was like he hadn't seen or heard us.

He brought the paper down, revealing his blue eyes, magnified through the lenses of his rubber-banded cat-eyed reading glasses.

"You boys shoot anything?" he said. "Where's all them rabbits at?"

"Lonnie fell into the ice. His dog wouldn't come and he went out there to get it and fell in."

"Well, son of a buck," Homer said, drawing it out, just truly realizing what happened.

Lonnie stared at the stove, shaking. It looked like he was about to cry. The Christmas tree was up in the corner, no lights, but decorated with acorn shells Granny had strung up with curling red-and-silver strips of tin cut from Homer's Prince Albert tobacco cans. They looked like tinsel.

"Eddie, go run Lonnie a bath," Granny said. "Lonnie, go into Eddie's room and get out of those clothes."

I ran hot water into the tub from a hose screwed into a faucet at the sink because the pipes under the bathtub had frozen. Granny laid out a towel and a pair of jeans and a sweater from my dresser drawer.

While Lonnie took a bath, my great-uncle said, "What's he crying around about?"

Over the years, I was always meeting one great-uncle or another, one of my grandma's six brothers. They were always big and tall and sort of intimidating, loud, but friendly, buying me pizza, pop, and baseball cards. They usually had some artwork for me to look at, visiting Granny and Homer out in the country from Tulsa.

But this one, Chester, I had never met before yesterday. He showed up the night before from California, showing me pictures of him in rodeos dressed up with a floppy cowboy hat, suspenders over a polka-dotted shirt, red tights under cutoff blue-jean shorts. With painted red circles on his cheeks, he wore high-top basketball shoes and waved the hat in a bull's face, inches from its horns. He had scruffed my head last night, playfully slap-boxing and tickling me until I was breathless. He said I'd never make it as a bulldogger unless I toughened up.

We piled into the car to take Lonnie home. Lonnie and I sat in back with Monkey Tail between us, his tail thumping the seat. Homer started the car and got out to scrape ice off the windshield as Chester, a former semipro football lineman, drank from his bottle in the passenger's seat, broad-shouldered and hunched over in the small sedan. Granny sat in the middle.

Chester turned and snatched Lonnie around the throat.

"You freaking n—!"

Lonnie's eyes grew big. He gripped the armrest beside him. Everything froze; snowflakes swirled and floated outside the window, slid down the glass. The little car rumbled, exhaust puffing from the tailpipe. The windshield wipers swished every few seconds, loud in the silence.

Chester's eyes were narrowed, his teeth bared in a sneer.

"Here now, Chester, leave him be! That's Eddie's friend," Granny said.

Monkey Tail grew tense in my arms, trembling, and let out a sharp bark at Chester.

One by one, second by second, the fingers released from around Lonnie's neck like in a countdown. The last one bore a turquoise ring.

Chester drank the rest of his bottle, rolled down the window, and flung it into the snow. Cold wind rushed in.

"Oh, heck, he knows I'd never hurt him," he said.

Lonnie looked at me wide-eyed. I mouthed "It's OK"—although I had no idea if it would be—and gave his shoulder a shake, keeping a wary eye on Chester, who had grown silent. It all happened so fast and without provocation, we didn't have time to react.

Chester instantly complied with Granny's wishes, which made me feel safer, but I kept watching him as he shivered, as though cold, pulled his cap over his eyes, and leaned back against the headrest. I was further relieved when Homer—oblivious to it all—got back in, revved the engine, and turned on the heater. Granny didn't say anything about it to him and, following her lead, I didn't either. It was best to let a sleeping dog lie. That sleeping dog didn't even know Lonnie. He didn't even know me, really, since I'd only met him last night.

Lonnie and I played with Monkey Tail on the ride down to the gate, making him snarl and yap. I got out and unchained the gate. We were quiet on the short ride to his place, past squat little houses with green shingling and pens and hutches nearby for pigs and chickens.

"Here, Lonnie, give these to your folks," Granny said, big jars of canned okra, small red potatoes, and cucumbers clinking in a box as she handed them over from the front seat. "Anytime you guys want more, come on over."

"Thank you very much, Granny, I'm sure Daddy's going to love this," he said. "Thanks for everything. You, too, Mr. Homer."

"See you later, Stud," Homer said. "We'll get them rabbits next time."

I got out with Lonnie and carried his sack of wet clothes to the front door.

"I'm sorry about all that, Lonnie, I don't even know him."

"Don't worry about it, it ain't your fault," he said.

We executed our ritualistic handshake, which ended with two quick back-and-forth claps and a finger snap. I walked back to the car.

"Chook."

I stopped and turned.

"Be careful," Lonnie said, and raised his jaw toward the car. I knew who he was pointing at.

With Lonnie gone, I didn't know if Chester would reach around and grab my neck next, so instead of going riding around with them, I said I wasn't feeling good and had Homer drop me back off at the gate. I walked up to the house through the pasture, past Chester's car in the yard with the California license plates I had thought were so exotic.

In my room, I got out my notebook and wrote down everything that had happened, from shooting at rabbits, the pups running and barking, and Lonnie falling in the pond. But from there, I rewrote it. Chester asked Lonnie if he was okay, where he lived, and what his parents did. He shook his hand and even boxed around a little with him, too. He took us to eat barbecue and bought us baseball cards. We went riding in the country to Fort Gibson Dam and saw eagles nesting in the bluffs. When we took Lonnie home he still had both pups, his gun, and rabbits to clean. But that was just a made-up story.

The next morning Chester sat at the table drinking coffee. I saw his unfamiliar silhouette through the sheet Granny hung up to keep the kitchen light out of my room. When I turned my fan off,

I could hear them talking and the radio playing softly. His voice sounded normal again. I regarded him warily for the few more days he was around, but never saw the hatred in his eyes again. He tried roughhousing and tickling me a few more times but I pulled away, picturing his hand around Lonnie's throat. After Christmas, he left. Granny said he'd gone back to California. I didn't see him again until his funeral a few years later.

I wondered if Lonnie would ever come back after what Chester did, and I wouldn't have blamed him if he didn't. I thought about which was more offensive: the name-calling or neck grabbing, and figured they were about the same, but even worse combined. I didn't see Lonnie again until weeks later. He yelled my name and slapped the open seat next to him when I got on the school bus for the first day of the new year. We talked about everything except what

Lonnie Hill, age seven, 1973.
(Courtesy of Melita Griffith.)

happened, it seemed. He even returned my clothes that he wore home that day. When spring came we started fishing again and in the summer he came over and we threw the ball against the pitch-back, angling it for grounders and pop-ups.

I never understood why Chester did that to Lonnie. Growing up, the N-word was not unheard of, but that was the first time I heard anyone say it with venom. Momma never said it. Homer and Granny, whose strongest word was "gosh," never used it. Muskogee schools were racially mixed but everyone on my bus home was Black except for me, my sister Dawn, and the driver, Mr. Anderson. The Native kids got along with the Black kids, and vice versa. Some of us were best friends, played on the same teams, and hung out after school. Some were even mixed, half-Black and half-Indian and members of a tribe, or had cousins who were, which made it harder for me to understand Chester's actions. Maybe it was his generation. But Homer's generation was even older and one of his oldest friends was a Black man in Tullahassee.

I had white, Black, Native, and Latino friends. I can't say I ever felt singled out or excluded from anything because of my race. Sometimes I found myself the only brown-skinned person in a setting, but I never felt ashamed or embarrassed. The city was more diverse than many small towns in Oklahoma where no Black or Indian people resided.

Nearby, small towns like Taft and Tullahassee ("Old Town" in Creek) were all-Black, but one sizable town, about fifty miles away outside of the Creek Nation, had zero African Americans. In the

1980s, a woman called from Philadelphia looking to relocate there and was told there were plenty of houses available. But when she arrived for a meeting to be shown properties, the agent saw that her adopted kids were from Ghana and suddenly there were no listings. That would have never happened in Muskogee, which always had substantial Native and Black populations—Black doctors, lawyers, and, I presume, real estate agents. Black students had their own schools in town until desegregation in 1970 when Manual Training and Central merged and Muskogee High School was born.

The riders on my bus were a blend of elementary, junior high, and high school students. I'd sit in back with Lonnie and slap out beats to songs on the backs of the high green seats along with everyone else. At first I never joined in, but when I finally did, Lonnie nudged his friend with an elbow and nodded his head in my direction as I pounded on the seats with everyone else. A boom box blared "I Wish." After a bass and keyboard intro, the vocalist sang about being a nappy-headed boy whose only worry was what would be his toy for Christmas.

The bus was packed three to a seat and ear-ringing loud with singing, arguing, laughing, and yelling. Mr. Anderson stopped on the side of the road and looked at us in the mirror with his owlish glasses and ball cap and said in a real friendly voice, "Now, boys and girls, we're going to have to keep the noise down."

"It ain't noise it's Stevie Wonder!" someone yelled.

The racket started up again but regressed in notches every time we dropped off a group down North 17th Street. It was quiet as a library by the time Lonnie got off. Dawn, Elaine Ledbetter, and I were the last to disembark after the asphalt ran out because the district didn't allow the bus down the dirt road. It turned around, empty, as we walked home. We all turned and waved to Mr. Anderson.

From the beginning of my school days in Muskogee, Black educators were a big part of my life. My first coach at age six, A. C. Richardson, played me at shortstop for the Blue Blazers, but would also put me on the pitcher's mound. I had two strikes on a batter one night at Hatbox Field and was about to deliver the next pitch, when I saw Momma in the stands behind the backstop pointing in the air. I stood on the rubber looking up into the sky until everyone started yelling throw the ball already. She told me later she was just holding up a finger to indicate one more strike.

Coach Richardson gave me the MVP trophy at season's end at the field where we practiced in Honor Heights Park. I had no idea it was coming, because I thought his son, Allyn, was our best player, but he called out "Chook" and gave me an Easton aluminum bat, silver with green letters, still shrink-wrapped in plastic.

Wearing my cleats, I dragged it to school every day, to the Muskogee Public Library, and back home. I don't know why I didn't carry it. I dragged it so much the rubber cap at the top fell off. Today you're probably not allowed to bring a bat or wear cleats to school— or to the library for that matter. I was so proud of that bat I should have had it bronzed.

At Jefferson in second grade, the only people who paid any attention to me were the older Black girls. They cupped their hands around my face while I watched them play tetherball and told me I was so cute. They asked what my name was and I said, "Radar," which I'd heard on the TV show *M.A.S.H.* I thought it was such a cool name. But they stuck me with Eddie Chocolate, Eddie Chickenlegs, and Eddie Spaghetti, following that with, "Got Your Meatballs Ready?" I hung around their periphery while they bashed the ball around the pole on a rope until they noticed me. I especially loved one girl named Velvet Lee.

CHAPTER 2

I PUT THE passage I wrote about Lonnie in a folder with my other writings. I wrote a lot out there in the country: stories I entirely made up and true accounts of things I'd seen or done at school. A sketch I wrote that Dawn and I performed for Granny and Homer used ripped-up newspapers for snow. I stood on a chair and tossed the shreds into the air. Dawn had trouble with some of the lines, but not with the action.

"OK, here's where you slap me," I said, also directing.

Before I could get the words out, she popped my face with a resounding smack.

"Ow, not that hard!"

Granny and Homer hooted from their chairs.

"Let's see that one again," Granny said.

Granny saved my first story, folding the notebook paper into an envelope in her wooden picture box. It featured the mountaineer cartoon character on the bottles of Mountain Dew pop that I drank all the time. Grinning in goofy celebration, he wore a floppy hat, patched-up pants, held a jug with a cork in it, and seemed to leap right off the bottle.

I wrote that he ran away from home; his family grew worried

and searched all day for him, finally finding him that night hiding in a tree. They all went home together and lived happily ever after. Not complex or layered with subplots, symbolism, and hidden meaning, but I was only seven years old.

Alone with Granny and Homer, I had a lot of time to write. After Momma divorced my dad, Donald "Shorty" Chuculate, when I was too young to remember, I usually stayed with them while Dawn lived with Momma. My visits with my Cherokee grandpa Ed were rare and he died when I was just eight years old.

In pictures he's stout and square jawed in suit and tie holding a Cherokee Bible. But my only recollection of him is a visit to his house

My grandfather, the Rev. Edward "Ed" Chuculate, in July 1957, forty-eight years old. Full-blood Cherokee, Ed was a barber and Baptist preacher who delivered sermons in Cherokee and English. One of his Bibles was printed in both languages. (Courtesy of the author.)

in Cherokee County, where he held a box-shaped device to his neck to help him talk after surgery for throat cancer. The mechanical-like vibrating noise was hard to understand and was usually interpreted for me by someone else.

I never called anyone "Dad" growing up. Homer and my stepdad, Roman Green, were my father figures. Momma married Roman when I was four years old, and I called him Roman. Homer I

My dad, Donald Everett "Shorty" Chuculate (left) and grandpa Delbert Ezell "Homer" Flanary, August 1967. I was two months shy of two years old, on a fishing trip. My dad told me he accidentally clotheslined me once while carrying me like this through a dark backyard. (Courtesy of the author.)

called "Homer." My first memory of my dad was seeing him in Tulsa when I was about twelve during court-ordered visitations.

At Granny and Homer's, I wandered the pastures in habitual solitude, fished for bullhead catfish in nearby ponds, batted my baseball into the fields and searched all over for it so I could slug it again, or shot at birds and rabbits with my BB gun. I discovered that white dandelion fuzz disappeared in a poof! with a direct hit. Sometimes Lonnie or my cousin Joe came to visit, but mainly I was alone.

It was cold in the winter mornings when we woke up because the fire in the stove went out during the night. You could see your breath in front of you. Always the early riser—and the first to go to bed—Homer usually had it going by the time I got up. But sometimes I'd start it.

You twisted open the handle to the iron door on front. If there was red glowing at the bottom of all the gray ash, you stirred it up with the iron poker so the coals were on top and got some air and came to life a little. If there was no life at all, you started from scratch with newspaper and a match.

Next to the stove, we kept a cardboard box of twigs, wood chips, bark, and branches—"kindlin'"—that you piled into it. If that didn't ignite you'd get on your hands and knees and blow until a tongue of flame leaped from the coals and licked the kindling. You waited until that got going, then laid in bigger limbs until they caught, then you added split, smaller chunks. If it was really cold you went out on the front porch and got a big log from the stack and crammed it in; it'd catch eventually.

You opened the circular vent on the bottom all the way to allow a good draft, then tamped it when the fire was roaring. When it was blazing, the stove glowed red. I'd stick my baseball cleats on the side, melting them down so Granny would have to buy me a new pair in the spring.

If the stove was too full of ash you opened a smaller door at the bottom and raked it out with the poker into a container that Homer salvaged from an old refrigerator, or "ice box" as we called it. These were the metal bins at the bottom used for fruits and vegetables. They're all plastic now. When that box filled you dumped it across the fence into the pasture, getting clouds of ash in your face and hair when the wind was wrong.

Homer also converted these bins into barbecues. The wire covers were coated in plastic, which burned off in a fire, and made a perfect grill. He hardly ever bought briquets; we had too much wood around, but Granny liked to go out in the country and round up pecan or hickory for fuel.

Before work in the greenhouse at Bebb's Flowers in Muskogee, she started her morning routine at the stove in her nightgown: bacon, eggs, biscuits, and coffee. For years I didn't think there were any other breakfast options. I didn't like milk so I never ate cereal. When my cousin visited she said it was the only time she saw a little kid drink coffee. I always added two spoonfuls from the sugar bowl on the table. Granny would snap on the radio and it seems "Country Bumpkin" would come on every time, the singer wondering how's the frost out on the pumpkin.

Granny could cook anything. The oldest of nine kids, she had grown up cooking for the family. She had a shoebox with recipes clipped out of magazines and newspapers, and on index cards written in her elegant cursive. In the spring we dug wild onions in spots Granny and Homer knew by creeks. The prime harvest season only lasted a few weeks. If the onions grew too tall or old they became tough. We'd pick a brown grocery sack full and sit around the kitchen table cleaning them, slicing off the hairy roots, peeling the top layers, and snipping the withered tops. A big sack like that cooks down to less than half its size.

Granny washed them off and steamed them with scrambled eggs in a cast-iron skillet. All Indians have their own recipes or think theirs are the best or the only way to cook them. Someone else's wild onions are too tough, too runny, have strange ingredients, the wrong grease, not enough eggs, too many eggs, or are served with the wrong side dishes. But you never complain.

Homer was Depression-era raised eating a lot of poke sallet and could spot the leafy, reddish-stalked plant growing roadside along ditches. He'd cut them off at the bottom with a knife and put them in a sack. Granny rinsed them, cut the stalks into rings, and sauteed them with the leaves in bacon fat.

She was the main cook for holiday feasts on Thanksgiving and Christmas, which was also Homer's birthday. She baked the turkey and ham, made stuffing from scratch and fresh ingredients, as well as gravy, mashed potatoes, and desserts like German chocolate cake and pumpkin, apple, and cherry pies. The smells began filling the house in the morning and lingered all day. Leftovers would be covered and left on the table and counters to be snacked on all day and reheated the next.

Granny could make meatloaf, spaghetti and meatballs, pork steak, fried chicken, and thick slabs of London broil–type beef bought at discount grocers that she roasted in a cast-iron skillet with garden-fresh carrots, onions, and potatoes. Her fried okra, fried squash, and fried green tomatoes were routine for me then but only delicacies now.

She made corn bread, skillet bread, and pancakes, sifting the flour in a metal shaker, and she cut out her biscuits with a tin ring. She used rolling pins to flatten the dough for pie crusts, sprinkling flour so the mixture wouldn't stick. Fried catfish, bass, and crappie were other specialties, the crust golden brown and the flesh white, flaky, and steaming. Homer didn't waste a morsel, stacking whole skeletons next to his plate. Chicken or fish from the trendiest restaurants always fails the Granny test. Meanwhile, Momma made a mean macaroni soup.

On special occasions we went to Slick's on Shawnee Bypass and 24th Street. Slick, an older Black man with white hair, served barbecue that he smoked with hickory in huts out back of the small restaurant. You could see and hear him chopping the brisket through a window behind the cash register. It was served with chunks of raw onion and tomato on wax paper. There were a few spots at the counter to eat and four or five tables with mismatched chairs. He had waitresses, but when it came time to pay, only Slick handled the money, appearing from the back wiping his hands on his white apron.

CHAPTER 3

WHEN GRANNY WENT to the store in the pickup, I was sure to be in it. It was a chance to get out of the hot house and into some cool air-conditioning in town. It was also a chance to pester her again to buy me the fancy water I'd seen in *Inside Sports* magazine: a green glass bottle, beaded with moisture, snowy mountains in the background. The water was "naturally sparkling," "bottled directly from a mineral spring," and "from France." French water had to be better than the regular old water we drank from the faucet.

Every time I'd ask her for it, she'd refuse. "You don't need that," she'd say. But she finally relented one day at the Safeway on West Okmulgee and 32nd. This is where we'd cash in the returnable pop bottles we found when we went riding around in the country on dirt roads. Dawn and I sat in the bed of the pickup while we meandered through the countryside and yelled "bottle!" when we saw one in a ditch. Homer would crawl to a stop and we'd scramble out to claim it.

I grabbed the green bottle off the shelf, and when I found Granny she was talking to a tall man in jeans and boots in one of the aisles. He towered over her. Putting the water in her cart, I heard them talking, but in Creek. I might have been able to understand some of the words if they talked slower. I looked up at him.

His sunglasses gave him a mysterious air, but his familiar tone with Granny made him unthreatening. He shook my hand when Granny told him I was her grandson. I heard her say "Hokte," which is "girl" in Creek, and Momma's family nickname. He smacked on gum and was always smiling. It was a short visit, and he walked away laughing and waving.

Outside, I asked who the man was.

"That was Tony Tiger."

"Tony Tiger?!" I yelled, instantly thinking of the TV commercial with the furry-striped feline who growled that Frosted Flakes were "gr-r-reat!" He became even more intriguing.

She said they were all raised together at West Eufaula Indian Baptist Church and he was friends with my great-uncles, her younger brothers. She hadn't seen him in years.

I unscrewed the cap off the bottle in the truck and took a big guzzle and immediately spewed it out the window. It tasted nasty, like chalk or baking soda. Before we left the parking lot I poured it out, money down the drain. Granny just shook her head. On the way home I couldn't stop thinking about meeting someone named Tony Tiger. I couldn't have known that years later he would take me to get my driver's license.

I was lucky, then, after wasting the water, that Granny bought me a baseball scorebook. I'd become fascinated by the one our coach, Jimmy Chitwood, used. He'd keep score with it pinned to a clipboard. Disgusted once with an umpire's call, he threw it down from his spot at the third-base coach's box and it speared the ground like a knife.

At nights I'd pull a kitchen chair up to the dresser in my room and keep score of Kansas City Royals games broadcast by KBIX-AM 1490 in Muskogee, listening on the GE clock radio. Following the instructions on the inside cover, I marked lines to the bases on the diagonal diagrams, checking off 1B for a single or 2B for a double, marking players' progress around the little diamond until they scored, when I blacked out the space with my pencil.

I also listened to Muskogee High School basketball announced by Larry Arnel on KBIX. But when they played at home Granny and Homer would drop me off at Roughers Gymnasium. I'd spy Arnel broadcasting the game from his perch on the second-level midway, sitting at a desk wearing headphones and speaking into a microphone. I'd sit behind him and listen. I saw him getting a pop at halftime and told him I listened to him on the radio. We didn't have a phone so Granny and Homer tuned in at home and picked me up when the game was over. If we ever had to make a call we drove into town to use the phone booth at the corner of 12th and Broadway.

CHAPTER 4

WITH JUST THREE channels, there wasn't a lot on TV for me, but I usually tuned in to *Mutual of Omaha's Wild Kingdom*, *The Undersea World of Jacques Cousteau*, and *Hee Haw*—musicians in a cornfield cracking jokes. I'd watch whatever Granny or Homer liked: *Benson*, *Barnaby Jones*, or *Barney Miller*. On *Maude*, starring Bea Arthur, they cut back and forth and a character suddenly had a different shirt on. I wrote in and won a "I'm a National Enquirer TV Blooper Spotter" T-shirt.

Sometimes I fell asleep on the couch and woke to KTUL-TV's sign-off of Southern Cheyenne artist Dick West doing the Lord's Prayer in Indian sign language. In full headdress, he made slow sweeping hand motions as the long fringes on his buckskin shirt swung in the breeze. My eyes fluttered to stay awake as he finished by slowly crossing his arms over his face, bowing his head.

I also had a portable record player that played 45s. It had a denim cover and folded over and locked in place like a little briefcase with a handle. The tiny speakers were built in on the sides and the cord stowed away inside. I stored both of my records in there: "Convoy" and "Stayin' Alive." I listened to "Stayin' Alive" over and over and copied down the words on notebook paper and sold the lyrics for a

Sixth grade at Riverside Elementary in Muskogee, 1978, age eleven. I flubbed and spelled "arithmetic" when asked to spell "mathematics" in the spelling bee finals. I should have asked for the word again. I didn't get the blue ribbon, but I spelled arithmetic correctly. (Courtesy of the author.)

quarter at school. Every time I made a sale I'd play the song over and over and write the stanzas down again. It never occurred to me to just write multiple copies or keep a master version.

Everyone had some kind of hustle going on in fourth grade at Houston Elementary. Bryan Greer made god's eyes out of yarn and two dowels that he sold for a quarter. Then he got fancy and used various colors and longer, multiple sticks at different symmetrical levels and upped the price. I used my lyrics money and bought a big diamond-shaped one in shades of purple that Momma hung on the wall. Students would bring candy and sell it at a profit. I never knew what was behind this retail craze. Then, some other kid started bringing lyrics to school and we'd argue over whose were more accurate.

In music, the teacher sat and banged out tunes looking at sheet music propped on the piano. We formed a semicircle in two rows behind her and sang "You're a Grand Old Flag" and "Rhinestone Cowboy," which always left me wondering what star-spangled rodeos were.

That year I had moved back into town with Momma at 1109 Fredonia in Muskogee in an upstairs apartment. I laid pennies on the nearby railroad tracks, stood to the side as the train rumbled by, and collected the coins that flattened into inch-long shapes.

Our Muskogee Knothole Association baseball team was the Kiwanis. After one game at Hatbox, Greer's mom volunteered to take a bunch of players to Chet's for chili dogs on West Okmulgee. We ate them in the car as we got dropped off at home all over town.

*Age nine, summer 1976, Kiwanis team picture day at Houston Elementary in Muskogee.
I idolized Pete Rose with this throwback to wool uniforms and wooden bats, but I didn't
model my stance after him. (Courtesy of the author.)*

They came on steamed buns wrapped in foil, dripping with chili, cheese, mustard, diced onions, and sweet relish.

Momma, returning from work at Teel Laundry, happened to be out front. Being friendly, the mothers waved and chatted briefly as I scrambled out the back, climbing over other players.

"He got a little bit on him," Greer's mom said as I exited with mustard and orange grease on my face and down the front of my uniform.

Mom was all pleasant waving bye.

Then, "Good lord! Look at you! Get up there and wash your dang face!"

Standing at the sink, I couldn't understand what all the fuss was about. Maybe she was embarrassed I was the only one who made a mess and it looked like she'd never taught me how to eat. But I had no experience eating messy hot dogs while riding over potholes in a crowded car.

Our Kiwanis team won about as many games as we lost, barely missing the playoffs. Our coach, Mr. Qualls, was from nearby Hulbert, and always brought two of our best players in his pickup, full-blood Cherokees Dinky and Zane. We also had two girls, Kim and Tina. They weren't too bad, either, just as good as some of the boys. It was embarrassing at first because we became known as the team with girls, but we got over it.

CHAPTER 5

WHEN I WAS four, before I started school or even heard of chili dogs, I lived with Granny and Homer in Hanna, a rural setting that made the outskirts of Muskogee look like a metropolis. In McIntosh County and the heart of the Creek Nation, Hanna was true isolation. The town itself was a few miles away and had only a gas station, post office, small general store, and bar. Neighbors we didn't know lived in faraway houses in pastures next to green fields of watermelons.

The house was on my great-great-grandpa Jackson Lewis's original Creek Indian land allotment, which had dwindled over the years from 160 acres to five, directly across the road from Hillabee Indian Baptist Church. For miles east or west, you could tell a car was coming by the plume of red dust it created on the dirt road before you actually saw or heard it.

My birth made five generations: Jackson, my great-grandmother Frances Narcomey, Granny, my mom, and me. Jackson was an old Creek Indian who didn't speak English but had a fair amount of money from land sales and gas and oil rights. He'd ride his horse all the way to Eufaula, twenty miles away, hitch it to a post on Main Street, and spend the night. Locals all knew his horse and that Jackson must be on a wild weekend again.

He'd sit in his chair in Hanna wearing a tan Stetson with a wide, circular brim and tall round crown, hands crossed over the hook of his cane, staring out the window with a frowning expression while everyone else watched TV. He had no interest in TV because he didn't understand what people were saying or doing on the screen.

They said as a baby I was making typical baby racket, crawling around his feet, yammering constantly. He piped up with "Inn-hey la!"—a Creek term for exasperation—at which Granny said I froze, staring at him in awe because it was the first noise I ever heard him make. A statue had just come alive.

There's a photo of the five of us in Hanna: Jackson in his wooden chair, staring ahead with a serious frown and ignoring the camera, with the next four generations standing around him looking at the photographer, Momma holding me in her arms.

My earliest first-person memory is of me on my hands and knees blowing into a small mound of pebbly red dirt in the front yard in Hanna, then running into the house and asking Granny, "If I blow into an ant hole, is it like a tornado for the ants?"

"Inn-hey la," Granny said, laughing, like she was wondering what question I'd come up with next. "I guess it would be. Go blow into another."

The term *Granny* may conjure images of canes, walkers, and hearing aids, but Granny was only forty years old. But by then she was already a grandma two times, and a couple years away from three. Even Momma and Homer called her "Granny" while she was "Mac" or Maxine to her brothers and sisters.

While some early memories were given to me in historical family

My birth made five generations. At front in 1968 in Hanna, Oklahoma, my full-blood Muscogee (Creek) great-great grandfather Jackson Lewis and his daughter, my great-grandmother Frances (Lewis) Narcomey. Behind her is Frances's daughter, my grandmother Maxine (Narcomey) Flanary. My mother, Lorencita "Lori" (Narcomey) Holmes, holds me. Jackson, who was eighty-seven years old here, was a man of few words, none of them English, which he didn't speak. He died in September 1969 at age eighty-eight. (Courtesy of the author.)

accounts, I distinctly remember blowing into the hole, wreaking devastation and EF-5 heartbreak upon the ants. My second physical memory is of collecting rocks from the dirt road in Hanna and firing them at a small white dog with a black splotch on his back that kept hanging around, and Homer saying the county commissioner was going to come looking for me for throwing away all his rocks. I thought he was serious, but he was just kidding. The dog hid under our porch and when he finally came out we adopted him: Spot.

I'd follow Homer into the woods behind the house and when I grew tired of walking he'd set me on his shoulders, high in the air with my legs dangling on his chest. We'd sit with our backs against the trunks, scanning the treetops for squirrels popping out of their nests or scurrying across branches and leaping limb to limb. It was fall and the squirrels were almost invisible among the gold and copper sycamore leaves, but you'd see a flash of movement and hear leaves rattle and twigs snap in the chilled air.

He'd fire and knock one down. I liked to handle the warm spent copper shell, smell the burnt sulfur, and blow into it and make it whistle. Homer had earned a sharpshooter rating in riflery in the army during World War II, but he never made it to combat because the war ended before he was shipped overseas.

"The Germans heard I was on my way," he always quipped.

I had three empty shells in my pocket on the way home; Homer carried three squirrels. He cleaned them, peeling off the furry hide like he was pulling it out of its clothes, down the legs like it was coming out of its pants. The bare flesh glistened red and milky blue.

Granny washed the meat under running water, coating the pieces in flour sprinkled with pepper, and fried them in a heavy cast-iron skillet. She fried potatoes with onion and made skillet bread. I had my meal with grape Kool-Aid. Homer ate the squirrel to the bone, chewing on the gristle. He never drank until he finished eating, then went to the sink and gulped one full glass of water, tilting his head back with a hand on his hip, Adam's apple bobbing.

Hunting was also a big Christmas tradition. We'd eat biscuits and eggs and drink coffee in the pickup as we rode down dirt country roads. I'd follow Homer through ditches, under and over barbed-wire fences, traipsing through fields where snow sparkled like jewelry and crunched beneath our feet. We were always on the lookout, stopping every so often to scan the horizon, shielding the sun with our gloved hands, breath fogging the air.

Sometimes our quarry was too big, or too small, and the hunt would continue until we spied the perfect specimen and Homer would withdraw his red-handled saw and cut it off at the base, green needles shaking onto his wool cap. We'd then reverse the trip, dragging the annual Christmas tree by its trunk across the fields, back to the truck and home, where we decorated it.

CHAPTER 6

I ALWAYS ANTICIPATED seeing cars and pickups arriving at the campgrounds across the road for weekend church services. Finally, there were other kids to play with and food to eat at the camphouses that surrounded the church. Over the long weekend, church families lived in these camphouses, squat structures with screened porches and windows that moths and locusts thumped into at night, attracted by light in the middle of the dark countryside.

We gathered water from the well by the bell near the church, removing the wooden lid and letting the tin bucket drop in a whir from the rope on a pulley, clanging against the brick sides before splashing on the surface, taking in water until it grew heavy and the rope tightened.

I was especially drawn to the camphouse used by Deacon Edmond Barnett, Jr., Thah-hah ("big brother") in Creek, the Rev. Austin Barnett's brother. He was tall and wore boots, jeans, and flannel shirts on Saturdays but a suit on Sundays. He had a deep voice and always treated me kindly.

"Where you been?" Granny asked me.

"At my camphouse."

"Oh, really," she said, tickled. "And which one is that?"

"Edmond's."

Granny and Homer didn't attend the church. She grew up as a preacher's daughter and by that time had had enough church. Her father, Raymond Narcomey, was among that generation of full-blood Indians who converted to Christianity and disapproved of traditions like stomp dancing. In that outlook, dancing around the fire was for heathens, even though he grew up doing it himself.

Stomp grounds weren't far from the church and beyond the trees, on occasion, you heard the singers chanting and turtle shells shaking, sometimes fast, sometimes slow. My great-uncles were punished if Raymond found out they had been stomp dancing, which can be religious or social, but they did it anyway. For years when I heard the term "stomping grounds," I thought it referred to stomp grounds.

In the morning after a night spent warm between Granny and Homer, I stood at the sink and shut my eyes and Granny washed my face with a hot soapy rag, scrubbing under my chin and behind my ears. She rinsed the rag until the water ran clear, wrung it, and repeated the process. At ten the church bell clanged in a slow rhythm and I crossed the dirt road with Dawn in tow, ducked under the shrubbery that formed a privacy fence, and went to Sunday school, taught by Austin's sister Maxine.

Then someone rang the bell again, and if it was too hot inside we assembled under an outdoor arbor with a slanted tin roof connected to the church. Otherwise, we went inside, where I marched down the center of the aisle and sat on a high-backed first-row bench, as close to Reverend Barnett as possible. Sometimes we went through a line and ate a little doughy wafer and drank a tiny cup of grape juice. I was always wanting more juice; it seemed like a lot of trouble for such a small taste.

I ate sofke at the church, a traditional soup-like Creek food made of corn and lye from wood ash. Our ancestors ate the nutritious staple in their homelands, and after the removal the tradition continued in Oklahoma. In the old days big kettles of sofke were left outside dwellings, and passersby and visitors ate from it using a wooden dipper.

The Rev. Austin Barnett (left) and his brother, the deacon Edmond Barnett, Jr., of Hillabee Indian Baptist Church. Shown here in Dustin, Oklahoma, in May 1978. (Courtesy of David Barnett.)

We sang hymns in Creek before Austin started his sermon. He had a wooden leg from a battlefield injury in WWII when he was taken prisoner by the Germans for five months, wore dark-tinted glasses, and spoke with a stern, frowning expression, sometimes closing his eyes, smooth pecan-colored hands clutching a Bible. He once told the congregation in Creek before beginning:

"I wish every one of you was like this boy here," he said, pointing at me. "He's here every Sunday, listening and paying attention, front row."

Not understanding Creek at four years old, I never knew what he'd said until one of his eight sons, Elliot, told me later. I was fascinated by the sounds that came out of Austin's mouth, much more melodious than English, and somehow more powerful and penetrating. If I didn't understand the true meaning of the words, then their music sang to me; they punctured the soul. I can still hear the rhythms of his speech to this day.

I'd go home and ask Granny what the words meant: Cesvs Klist (Jesus Christ), laksetv ("to tell a lie"), este-nekrivc ("the devil"), and fvtceckv-net (Judgment Day). I misspoke them in the wrong accents, I'm sure, but Granny gave it her best translation. I wrote the terms and definitions down in a notebook. Granny later told me the Creek kids were slapped on the hands with a ruler if they talked Creek in class at public school in Eufaula, but they spoke it among themselves anyway at recess. I pictured Granny standing in a corner in a classroom and wondered if the same would happen to me. I hadn't started school yet, but I'd heard from my older cousins of the spankings you'd get. I just didn't know they were with a wooden ruler.

When I heard Granny and Great-Grandma Frances speaking Creek at the kitchen table, I joined them with my notebook, peppering them for the words to everyday objects: chicken (delozy), cat (bozy), raccoon (wotko), rain (oske), sunshine (hvsotte), skunk (kona), and tornado (hotvule rakko, or "great wind"). I also learned to say jebon (boy), jissie (mouse), loja (turtle), katcha (tiger), and jitto (snake). I'd write the words down until they shooed me away to continue their conversation.

"Inn-hey la," Granny would say. "Go out yonder and play."

CHAPTER 7

I LEFT HANNA after a year when I was five to start school and live with Momma and my stepdad, Roman, in Calera in southern Oklahoma, about two hours south. Roman was Chickasaw and his family lived there: his mom; dad; sisters; and brother, Roston. Roston had four kids, one of whom, Bud, was my age. Bud became my cousin, and Roman's parents became Grandma Green and Grandpa Green.

Before my first day of school, we visited Roston, who had a brick house at the edge of town next to a rural area where he owned a few acres of land. They had some horses and saddled their most gentle riding horse for the kids to ride. I petted the horse on its long nose, rubbing the spiky rust-colored hair, while Roston's daughter Nancy mounted up. Bud delicately fed it a whole red apple. Its teeth looked like yellowed dominoes as it crunched the apple. I jerked my hand away from its nose.

"He won't bite," Bud said. "But I wouldn't stick my fingers in there."

With Nancy atop, the horse walked slowly away from the front yard, where everyone had gathered, and through a gate out into the pasture. Nancy's ponytail bobbed as she loped along in a meadow filled with yellow wildflowers. She made a wide circle like on a racetrack and let the horse stop and eat grass, its neck arched to the ground and black tail swinging. She trotted back, and when the horse hit the cement driveway its hooves clopped. It snorted and swung its head as Nancy dismounted.

"Eddie's turn!" they all yelled.

The horse stood docile as Bud fed it another apple, but its skin rippled and twitched, its tail slapped at a fly on its rump, it lifted a hoof, then set it down. A stationary object vibrating with motion.

Nancy rubbed its sides with a brush. "Good boy," she said.

I had never ridden a horse but didn't have any qualms about it, having watched everyone else. I walked behind it and Roston said, "Don't walk right behind him, he might kick."

As soon as he said that the horse kicked out a leg in a quick blur, still chomping on the apple. The second thing I did wrong was step into the opposite stirrup. You're supposed to place your foot in the left stirrup and swing your right leg over. I walked back around in front and Nancy helped me on.

I was way up in the air. I gripped the horn of the saddle as Nancy handed me the reins.

"Just pull back on these if you want to make him stop," she said, then, to the horse, made a clicking noise inside her mouth. The horse began walking. I jostled back and forth slowly on the hard saddle.

But instead of walking through the gate into the pasture, he veered right and began trotting down the gravel road toward a small bridge at the bottom of a hill near town. He gathered speed as I looked back toward Momma and the others in the yard.

"Pull! Pull!" Roston yelled with his hands cupped around his mouth, then made a jerking motion. "Pull on the reins!"

I pulled as hard as I could, but the horse only went faster, gathering speed as I leaned back on the leather straps. I thought I was going to fall off. Soon, we were galloping along the gravel road and all I could do was hold on. My cap blew off and I yanked again with all my might on the reins, but the horse flew like the wind, which roared in my ears. We neared the wooden bridge, which had no rails, and the water of a small creek rushed at me as my whole body bounced, shaking my vision.

I was still pulling on the reins when it slowed to a stop on the bridge. The water didn't look deep but it looked far away. I thought the ordeal was over, but even as I tugged on the reins the horse took off again across the bridge and up the hill, slinging me backward. I held on. It loped off the road as a car approached, jumped a ditch, and I felt my butt leave the saddle.

It stopped to eat a clump of weeds, ripping them out at the roots. I thought about jumping off, but looking down it felt like I was on top of a two-story building. It was as if the horse thought it was without a rider and was doing whatever it pleased. Maybe I didn't weigh enough. I obviously didn't have enough force with the reins.

It turned around on its own and walked back down the ditch and onto the road. By this time Roston and Roman had caught up, and Roston led it back to the house with me still on top, the horse gentle again. My heart thumped like a caged rabbit. I didn't want to talk or move for fear of spurring the horse into action.

"Don't know what got into him," Roston said.

Roman laughed. "Heck of a first ride," he said.

After I climbed down with my legs shaking, I had to admit it was scary fun. But I declined any future horse rides. I'd rather ride a bike. When Bud and I went exploring out in the pasture, I always looked for the horse and could spot it instantly among the others. I felt like we had a certain connection.

CHAPTER 8

MY FIRST DAY of school started off well enough in Calera—it was my first year of public education as Granny and Homer had homeschooled me in Hanna, and they taught me basic math, reading, and spelling in lieu of kindergarten or Head Start.

"Can anyone tell me what time it is?" was the first question Mrs. Parker asked us after introducing herself, pointing above the blackboard.

I looked around at the other kids. Some stared at the clock, at their desks, or out the window. The room was full of pictures and drawings of birds and bears, dogs and cats, and tons of books of different colors and shapes in bookcases and stacked on desks. No one said a word. I waited until the second hand clicked one more notch until it was straight up.

"Eight-thirteen," I said.

Mrs. Parker looked surprised, then peeled off a sticker from a pad on her desk and came over and stuck it onto my red Big Chief writing tablet. Homer had taught me to read a clock in Hanna.

"Eddie gets a gold star for today," she said.

After a brief lesson on how to tell time, she brought out a long, thick paddle from a metal cabinet and laid it on her desk. It looked big as a boat oar. It was certainly bigger than the wooden rulers I'd heard about.

"Don't worry, kids," she said in a very pleasant voice, noticing our reactions, "this is only for the bad boys and girls."

I'd been switched or spanked with a belt a few times but had never seen a paddle before and it terrified me. If a skinny tree branch peeled of its twigs could have me leaping and howling in the yard like I'd been stung by red ants, what pain would a board made from the same tree inflict? I figured even a gold star couldn't protect me from it.

Before noon we lined up at the door and marched single file to the cafeteria for lunch. But as we neared the school's main double-door entrance down the hallway on the way to the lunchroom, I

With Granny and Momma around 1970 in Hanna at the house across from Hillabee Indian Baptist Church. I didn't just have a football, I wore a jersey over shoulder pads. (Courtesy of the author.)

peeled off and exited, then strolled the three blocks to our house. I'd tell Momma about the beating I feared from Mrs. Parker and her paddle.

The screen door was locked but I could see Momma in the kitchen, standing over the stove in shorts and sandals, wearing a blue bandana on her head like a bonnet. I rattled the door.

"Eddie, what are you doing here? You're supposed to be in school!"

"Lunch," I said, stepping in.

"I thought you were supposed to eat at school!"

I thought she'd be glad to see me. But her tone made me worry I'd get the same spanking here I feared from Mrs. Parker. Even though Roman's belt was currently around his waist while he was at work, there was a backyard full of tree branches, so I hushed up about the paddle and Mrs. Parker.

I took my seat at the kitchen table while she made me a pickle loaf sandwich and bowl of macaroni soup. The night before at dinner Roman had asked me to read the bottom of the pepper can. They were always asking me to read things. It said *Nt. Wt. 5 Oz.*

"Nitwit five oz?" I said, supplying my own vowels, and didn't understand why Roman laughed and laughed, asking me to repeat it.

I ate while Momma got dressed. She drove me back to school. I was greeted at the main entrance by a fellow first grader who opened the door with a worried look.

"Mrs. Parker's looking for you! You're going to get that paddle!" he said.

Momma waved and drove away as I entered the building.

"No, I'm not!" I said, noticing a matching set of double doors across the hallway, which led to the playground and ball fields. I ran straight for those and began my existence as a first-grade fugitive, leaving my classmate behind, pointing and gawking. I saw him run down the hallway to find Mrs. Parker and tell.

I banged through the back doors, ran under some trees in the park, and went to the baseball field and hid in the dugout, wondering what to do.

I couldn't go back home; they'd be looking for me there. I couldn't go to Bud's; that would be the next place they looked. Granny and Homer's in Hanna was too far; it would probably take me hours to get there and I didn't know the way.

I could just wait on this wooden bench littered with sunflower seed shells and go home around three like nothing happened. It'd be a long wait, but I thought I could do it. As I wondered what to do, I began to hear a loud tangle of excited voices in the distance, growing near.

I took off running along the outfield fence and disappeared into the trees. I could go to Shane Sexton's for a while. I had been there last week with Roston and Bud and thought I could find it again. I waited a few more minutes, lying in the tall grass, then struck out for Shane's, determined to find the long white trailer with a white doghouse out front and green truck in the driveway. Shane wouldn't be there, of course; he was in class, where I should have been, in Mrs. Parker's first-grade room.

I found Shane's and rapped on the door. I was so short his mom looked out the curtains and right over my head, not glancing down until I knocked again.

"Eddie, what on earth are you doing here?" she said, opening the door for me to come in. "Why aren't you in school? Where's Shane?"

"I left early." Not untrue.

I sat at her kitchen table, and she brought me a saucer of cookies and glass of milk.

She sat down across from me and asked again about school and Shane. I said that he was still there, I had gotten out early, and could I just wait on him here? She told me to finish my cookies as she got on the phone, speaking in hushed tones and glancing my way. I heard my name spoken.

I put the last two cookies in my pocket and ran out the door. The bulldog in the next yard, chained to a stake in the ground, banged against the fence, barking at me.

I saw a group of older kids walking down the street, so I stuck to the ditches on the side of the road and crawled into a tinhorn culvert, where I heard them pass. I ate the last of the cookies and daydreamed while planning my escape.

I was startled by dogs barking, filling the tunnel with thunderous, echoing howling. A voice yelled, "I found him! Got him right here! Hey, kid, you OK? Come on out of there!"

I froze, not knowing what to do, thinking of the paddling from the boat oar I would get from Mrs. Parker at school, then a spanking from Momma at home. I felt a tugging on my jeans and began to slide out. An older kid was pulling me by the pants legs, and I relented as he stood me up and brushed dirt and twigs off my face, the dogs barking and tugging their leashes.

A meeting was held that afternoon at school with the principal, the police chief in uniform with boots and hat, me, Momma, and Mrs. Parker. The entire twelfth-grade class had been let out to search for me, in what was probably considered an exciting break from the first day of school by the seniors.

One student had driven home and retrieved his dogs and hit the trail with them. They tracked my scent from the front of the school, out the back, around the block, and to the baseball field, to Shane's trailer and down the road to the culvert. There was a picture of him with the dogs in the newspaper the next day.

I told them I had been afraid of being spanked by Mrs. Parker and her paddle, which brought her to tears, and she hugged me, and we both started crying. She vowed to never paddle me and said she'd put it out of sight. Momma didn't spank me, either, at home. When Roman came home from work that evening, he just laughed when told of my escape.

With the paddle locked back up in the cabinet, I never saw it again and it gradually drifted from my mind. Nevertheless, I tried my hardest for gold stars every day, and by the end of the year my Big Chief tablets were covered with them—shields against a paddling, I figured.

I wasn't spanked in school until third grade at Franklin Elementary in Muskogee, another change in what became a lifetime's chain of transition, different schools almost every grade until high school, but then I didn't even cry.

CHAPTER 9

WE MOVED TO Muskogee before I finished first grade. About three hours north, it was Momma's hometown, and she and Roman both got jobs at Coburn's Manufacturing. I now had a new baby brother, Anthony, who was born in Durant before we moved.

I walked home from Jefferson Elementary, a half-mile route that took me four blocks west and two south. One afternoon I saw a red purse hanging in the bushes next to a house. I dug through it and found a pack of gum, the kind that leaks liquid when you bite into the middle. Chewing on two or three pieces, I brought the purse home to Momma. After we returned it using the address on the ID Momma found inside, the woman thanked me profusely on her front porch, but I was terrified she'd discover the pieces of her gum missing.

Dawn and I were home alone from around three thirty to five fifteen when Momma returned from work. Momma made us memorize the address and phone number: 320 South 15th, 687-3390. I was just tall enough to reach into the mailbox on the porch and get the key when I got home from school.

We watched *Uncle Zeb's Cartoon Camp* from three thirty to four and argued over what shows to watch next, *Leave It to Beaver* or *Looney*

Tunes with Foghorn Leghorn and the chicken hawk. For a sad two weeks there was nothing on but men in suits sitting behind microphones during the Watergate hearings. So, we played in the fenced-in backyard with our German shepherd, Butch, or I ventured up and down the weedy alley behind the house, but I wasn't supposed to.

I also probably wasn't supposed to climb on the house. But I discovered by scaling the chain-link fence near the back porch I could easily reach the roof. I showed Dawn this, and she was able to get up there, too, even though she was only in first grade. But instead of descending back down the fence, I jumped from the low-hanging back-porch roof. It was easy enough. So when Dawn began to climb down the fence, I stopped her.

"Jump off like I did," I told her.

She bent at the knees on the precipice, arms in front and tongue out in concentration as if about to plunge off a diving board. I urged her on. She finally leaped, dress billowing, and landed in a heap. She cried and grabbed her leg. I helped her into the house and ran a bath and dumped Epsom salt into it, like I'd seen Granny and Momma do. I must have thought Epsom salt was a cure-all right up there next to penicillin.

When Momma came home, she asked where Dawn was.

"Taking a bath," I said.

It wasn't even five thirty, way before bath time.

She found Dawn in the tub, sweating and crying. They took her to Muskogee General Hospital, and she returned in crutches and a cast on her broken leg. I guess the way Dawn told it, I made her jump off, which I didn't think was necessarily the case.

Me, Momma, and little sister Dawn in Hanna, around 1970. Dawn and I would attend church services on weekends directly across the road at Hillabee Indian Baptist Church. (Courtesy of the author.)

I thought Momma might whip me with Roman's belt, but she only sat me down and explained I wasn't going to be allowed to play my first season of Paul Young peewee football as punishment. The games hadn't started yet, but I had been to a few practices. I wasn't exactly devastated by this; I liked baseball better anyway.

We had a set of *Encyclopædia Britannica*, twenty-four heavy, numbered volumes in red leathery covers shelved in two rows of twelve in a wooden case in the corner. I don't remember where they came from or who bought them, they were just there one day.

I'd lug one of these down at random, trying to comprehend at eight years old lengthy articles on Indian tribes, the Warsaw Pact, or anatomy. That section contained glistening, overlapping transparent layers that revealed more of the body every time you turned the page, starting with just the skeleton and finishing with the heart, kidneys, brain, and other organs.

The billiards entry contained colored diagrams of slender cue sticks and bridges, and pictures of long tables covered with red felt and diagonal racks of blue and yellow balls. The balls I thought peculiar because they were solid colored without numbers, unlike the ones on our Pivot Pool set, which had a stationary swiveling mechanism with which you'd fire the little white cue ball in a miniature version of eight ball. We'd clear off the kitchen table and set it in the center. In an odd switch, it was Roman who was always up for a Pivot Pool game, while I was the one with my head stuck in an encyclopedia.

My sister "Missy," or Melissa, was born two years after Anthony, who was now big enough to climb the backyard fences. When he did this, Butch would snatch him by the rear and yank him back. This is my earliest recollection of Anthony: a bowlegged, dark-skinned baby walking around the house with his diapers shredded because Butch was always foiling his escape attempts. Butch knew not to bite his legs or arms, just gentle-jawed tugs at his Pampers.

We couldn't find Anthony one day after searching all over the house, even on top of the refrigerator and in cabinets and closets because he was such a climber. I even checked the roof. Roman walked the streets, around the block, up and down the alleys, yelling out, *"Anthoneeeeee! Anthoneeeeee!"*

Finally, they called the Muskogee Police Department. They said they had a little, brown-skinned bowlegged boy right here wearing ripped-up diapers. When Roman picked him up at the downtown station, he told us Anthony was sitting high on a counter, swinging his legs and eating an ice cream cone like he was right at home.

An officer had seen him walking down a sidewalk along 15th Street and brought him in. He couldn't ask him where he lived, I guess, because Anthony was only two. He figured someone would be missing him soon enough. Anthony had managed to slip past all of us, even Butch.

CHAPTER 10

AT SCHOOL WE received the *Weekly Reader* and every couple months or so took a catalogue home to order books. I'd agonize over my decisions because I had only a few dollars to spend. I'd tally up my selections, erasing, adding, and subtracting the new totals, always overshooting my limit, hoping Momma would give in and let me order more.

She'd give me a few dollar bills and scrape up change for my choices, which I took to the teacher. Weeks later, when I'd forgotten about it, I'd walk into the classroom in the morning and there'd be stacks of boxes by the teacher's desk. The books were in!

When they were unpackaged and we were called up to retrieve our orders, some kids had towering stacks on their desks, but I was always satisfied with my three or four because I had another outlet: the Muskogee Public Library. It was right across the street from Jefferson and on the way home every day I stopped in like it was a continuation of school, dragging my bat.

The children's section was downstairs in the newly built library, which was clean and cool with palms and water fountains in the corners and under the stairs. The tile in the entryway and front concourse was always gleaming. There was an elevator, too, but it went up to the adult section, where kids weren't allowed. The tall windows were tinted and looked dark from the street outside. You could see out, but people couldn't see in.

I'd read entire books or listen to stories on albums. You'd check out headphones and sit at desks with built-in record players. I listened to one over and over about a Black boy going to school on a train in the big city of Chicago. I was fascinated by the sounds of the train rumbling, the noise of traffic when he got off, and the lingo they spoke at school.

Browsing the books, I found I'd already read a lot of them that interested me, including all the books on Babe Ruth. You wrote your name on cards in the pockets on the insides of the books when you checked them out, and I showed Alice Moschak, the children's librarian, that my name appeared several times on all the Ruth biographies. She let me follow her upstairs into the magical adult level and into the 796 Dewey decimal section of sports.

She pulled a few titles out, thumbing through them, and handed me one she thought suitable: a small red library-bound edition that said simply *Babe Ruth* in gold letters. I couldn't just sit down and rip through this one; I actually had to check it out and take it home. After that, as far as I knew, I was the only kid allowed upstairs without a parent.

Sometimes the bookmobile drove down our street and parked in the summers. It was a big van but smaller than a school bus. Kids and adults lined up outside to step in and check out and return books. For me it was just as exciting as the ice cream truck, only you didn't have to listen for the tinkly music and chase it down the street waving a dollar bill.

I also waited on the church bus on Sunday mornings to go to Temple Baptist across town. After Sunday school I sat in the main congregation, and after a sermon the preacher began asking people to come up around a tank of water. Following them, I walked down the aisle and stood in line. When it was my turn, the preacher cradled my head with the back of his hand. I closed my eyes and he leaned me back and dunked my head under. People were clapping when I came up.

I told Momma at home that I'd been baptized, having no idea what it meant. It wasn't planned, so there wasn't a big celebration or anything. I thought, *Well, that's that. Do I keep going to church now that I'm baptized? Does it last forever or do I do it once a year or something?* I went to church at Hillabee mainly because it was a chance to see other kids once or twice a week and it was right across the road. And after we moved from 320 South 15th, I fell out of the Sunday school routine and church never became a habit.

Around this time, when I was seven or eight years old, Roman got me my first job. He ran a filling station on weekends just outside Fort Gibson, opening the store and pumping gas. Momma thought it'd be a good idea if I went along and helped out. Either that or she just wanted me out of the house.

This was when most stations in Oklahoma were full service, meaning someone would come out when you drove up and put gas in your tank. You didn't even have to get out, you just paid the attendant, who usually also cleaned off your windshield.

I rode with Roman over the Arkansas River bridge that separated the two towns. Sometimes you'd see long barges underneath arriving or departing the Port of Muskogee, heading for the Mississippi River. Across the bridge on the south was the Oklahoma Gas & Electric facility, where Roman worked during the week and which at night to me looked like a futuristic city, sprinkled with orange lights. He captured a pair of wild bunnies there when we picked him up from work one day, bringing them to the car. We kept them in a box with grass in the backyard, but they escaped overnight and were gone the next morning.

At the small station just off the highway, I'd dip the squeegee into the tank of blue water and run around trying to clean all the windows while Roman pumped gas and checked oil. It was hard to do without leaving lines or smears on the glass, and I usually just made a mess of things and Roman had to finish up. I finally pestered him enough until he said he'd let me pump gas.

A bell dinged in the office when someone pulled up, running over a black hose on the driveway. I followed Roman out and he showed me the routine. I didn't really pay attention; I knew it all anyway. You just put it in and squeezed the trigger.

An elderly gentleman drove in later and said he wanted "two dollars regular." I hurried, wanting to do the whole job myself before Roman came to help.

"Yessir," I said, circling to the rear of his sedan.

"It's on the side there, son," the man said out the window, hooking an arm and pointing with his finger after he saw me hunting all around the trunk.

Already flustered, I twisted off the gas cap, which made a little hiss, removed the horsehead from the pump, and turned a small lever that reset the meter of gallons pumped to zero. I inserted the nozzle into the hole and squeezed, heard the gas rush out. I'd seen Roman lock a little lever that allowed the contraption to run on its own while he aired up a tire, collected money, or chatted with the driver. I locked it in place. The numbers inside the glass spun.

Roman was at the register ringing up a couple of customers buying fishing licenses. He looked out and I waved. A train rumbled by in town and vehicles began lining up at the crossing, some towing boats heading for the lake.

The gas nozzle clicked and jumped and gas came gushing out, spilling down the side of the car.

"Good God, kid, what have you done?" the man said, now standing next to me.

I had been daydreaming, I guess, proud of the job I was doing. We stood looking at the puddle forming around the rear tire.

"What's going on?" Roman said.

I stood aghast, looking up at the two men.

"I told him two dollars and it looks like he overfilled it. I was about on empty!" he said.

I thought Roman would be mad, but he just laughed and wiped the gas off the car with the orange rag he wore stuffed in his back pocket. He replaced the cap and rehung the nozzle.

The customer was a friendly old guy, and he and Roman stood around laughing at my expense.

"His first day on the job," Roman told him. "Looks like you got you a full tank for two bucks today, mister!"

"Thank you, sonny!" He gave me the money, then shook my hand.

I had a feeling the man felt guilty about all the free gas, but he did say he only wanted two dollars' worth. Gas was exactly fifty cents a gallon then.

CHAPTER 11

I SPENT THE summer with Granny on 17th Street in the country. Granny never went to college, but she was bilingual—speaking Creek and English—and played the piano and sang. She won spelling bees in school and had perfect attendance. She also corrected my pronunciation of words. My baseball book said a new team was joining the major leagues, the Seattle Mariners. I told Granny this, pronouncing them the "MARINE-ers," like the US Marines.

"That's MAR-i-ners," she said.

I read to her from my Cub Scouts manual about how to earn a "photo-GRAPHY" badge.

"It's pho-TOG-raphy," she said, enunciating.

Granny overheard me making fun of Homer, in a stunning display of hypocrisy, because he pronounced aluminum "ALOOMI-num," which, frankly, is what it looks like on paper if you think about it. Granny sat me down and told me not to make fun of Homer. He never got to finish school, she said. He went to work in the fields picking cotton when he was only twelve years old and still works hard every day to feed us, she told me.

Homer read the *Muskogee Phoenix* in its entirety every day— even the want ads, public notices, and the little print in sports. The paper listed criminal activity under "Police Reports," incidents of burglaries, vandalism, or assaults when police had responded. Every day in tiny type someone was getting spat on, kicked, or cracked over the head with a bottle.

If Homer was watching sports on TV or reading the paper you always had to repeat yourself if you asked him a question. It would go unanswered for a long stretch, then he'd reply with an absent-minded, drawn-out "Whaaaat?" still reading the paper. I sometimes forgot what I had asked. So engrossed in the games, he'd flinch or make body motions sitting in his chair along with the action like he was trying to stay in bounds or avoid getting hit with a pitch. One of my earliest baby pictures shows me standing on his lap poking around at his face as he watched a game.

He announced headlines from his living-room chair. You'd look but only see the paper being held wide open before him. His opinions on matters were things as he saw them "in my books."

"Pete Rose hit a home run, I see," Homer told me one morning, folding up the paper and taking off his glasses. I had already read it and saw no mention of a Rose home run.

I found the story and read it again, seeing nothing on my favorite player.

"No, he didn't. Doesn't say anything about it," I said.

"Let me see that thing," Homer said, quickly ruffling through the pages, skipping the story itself and handing me a page containing a blizzard of tiny numbers and letters. "Right there. Can't you see?"

He pointed to the small type in the box scores. After scanning a confusing array of Xs and Os and incomprehensible abbreviations, I still didn't see it. Nothing about a home run.

"Are you blind, Hoss?" he said. I followed the tip of his index finger yellowed from Prince Albert cigarettes to the tiny letters: HR—Rose (6).

"HR. Home run," Homer said.

"So he hit six in one game?"

"No, that's how many he's got all season."

Homer acted like everyone should know how to read a box score, no matter if you were only nine years old.

My great-grandma Frances dubbed me Jbacke, "mad" or "angry" in Creek, for antics I got away with around Granny and Homer but not Momma. A fish pulled in my entire rod and reel while I wasn't paying attention at Taft Lake. I looked up just in time to see the whole rig slide into the water and vanish. I stomped up and down the bank, throwing rocks into the water, getting into the truck, and slamming the door. I carried on until they drove me back into Muskogee and bought me another Zebco 33 combo at Kmart and returned to the lake.

I left my leather baseball glove outside on the porch and it rained all night. It weighed about ten pounds when I put it on the next morning. I stormed through the house, whining and kicking at things, pouting and refusing to talk like it was their fault it had stormed overnight. But I knew they'd buy me another one because I had a game in Fort Gibson that evening.

We stopped again at Kmart on the way, and they bought me

a plastic composite version because a solid leather model was too expensive. I grumbled about this as well, but Homer said my real glove would dry out in a day or two. Covering third from my shortstop position in the final inning, the ball popped out of the slick, stiff glove and the winning run was scored. Of course, I blamed it on the stupid mitt.

Momma didn't tolerate such tantrums, so I never even tried. But even Granny had her limits. I was always bugging her to buy more BBs. She was constantly busy doing something around the house or garden, but I expected her to drop everything and drive into town for more BBs at that instant. I don't remember the specifics of the argument, but I said something that set her off and she went into my room, grabbed my gun, and in a rage shook all the BBs out onto the kitchen floor. I stood there aghast, never seeing her react like that, hair hanging over her face. I knew I'd crossed an invisible line. Later she swept them into a dustpan and gave them back.

Returning from Taft Lake on a Sunday night, I had caught one largemouth bass, big enough to keep, but nothing to mount on the wall. Homer had been "skunked," as he called it, catching no fish. Mine was on a stringer in the back of the truck in an ice chest of lake water. I was living with Momma then, going to Franklin in third grade, and I had spent the weekend with Granny and Homer.

Momma met me at the door on the porch in curlers and a nightgown, waved at Granny and Homer.

"What are you doing with that thing?" she said.

"Going to eat it," I explained.

"Not tonight. You need to take a bath and get in bed for school tomorrow. I'll fix you a sandwich."

I threw another fit. She yelled back at me, told me to get my rear in the tub. The fun and games of that day with Granny and Homer at the lake were clearly over. I sat in the tub pouting, heard Momma bang pans around in the kitchen, still yelling.

When I came out in my nightclothes, she was smoking a cigarette in the kitchen, scowling. On the table in the center of a white plate lay the freshly fried fish, its golden-brown tail fin curled in the air.

Granny and Homer with me crossing my arms; my brother, Anthony Green; and youngest sister, Melissa "Missy" Green, dwarfed in the middle, circa 1977, in Muskogee. (Courtesy of the author.)

"Now eat the dang thang," she said.

The smiley face on the yellow plastic drinking glass mocked my frown. I'd gotten my way, but now Momma was mad and I'd lost my appetite. And she'd only get angrier the longer I waited. Granny may also have balked at cooking so late, but I realized I would have accepted her decision with no fuss. What, then, was the difference? As I picked up my fork I thought about complaining that Homer always cut the fin off, but a look at Momma's face shut me up. I ate.

CHAPTER 12

THE LIBRARY BECAME a second home to me. Granny would drop me off afternoons on Saturdays and pick me up when it closed at seven. She surprised me one Saturday, showing up early. I saw her in the lobby. She said Homer was watching the baseball game on TV and Pete Rose was closing in on 3,000 hits. We hurried home to see Rose slug his third home run of the day against the Mets for his 2,996th career hit. He didn't reach 3,000 until the next Friday, but we couldn't watch it since it wasn't a Saturday afternoon or Monday night game—the only times networks broadcast games.

I spent summer hours alone watching American Legion baseball games at the old Bacone College field. Games so obscure there were literally no fans. Just players and umpires and maybe a guy sitting in the press box. The *Phoenix* covered the team, so I knew when there were home games, usually a midweek or Saturday afternoon doubleheader. It was always a day game because there were no lights.

Granny and Homer would drop me off and I'd sit in the bleachers wearing my plastic Cincinnati Reds batting helmet or wander down by the fence next to the dugout. When they took me to my first game as a toddler, they said I ran terrified from the backstop when the catcher walked back to retrieve a ball, looking like a towering monster in his mask, chest protector, and shin guards.

But now I liked to look at the players with black smudges under their eyes and all their gear: rags of sticky pine tar, rolls of flesh-colored tape they strapped around their wrists, weighted "donuts" for the silver-green Easton aluminum bats, high-dollar Wilson A2000 leather gloves, and batting gloves hanging like rabbit ears from back pockets.

I watched them spit sunflower seeds, dip Skoal and chew Levi Garrett, or chomp giant wads of gum, blowing pink bubbles as big as balloons that popped and plastered to their faces. I loved to hear the metal scrape of spikes on cement because in our Midget level of Knothole ball we wore plastic cleats.

It looked like the pitchers were standing on mountaintops and throwing 100 miles an hour. The ball left the pitcher's hand whip-like in a long white blur, zipping through the air with a hiss, popping the catcher's mitt like a rifle shot, puffing dust. I didn't see how anyone could hit anything thrown so fast.

As soon as I'd think that, a batter would connect with a loud clank! The guys would come out of the dugout in a line with their heads craned in the air, watching the ball soar high into the chalk-blue sky until it disappeared with a splash into the leafy-green trees beyond the outfield fence.

Those balls I didn't bother to pursue. But the ones that sprayed behind the tall backstop I chased down like a bird dog. Unlike at Little League games, there was no competition here for the foul balls and ensuing free pop or snow cone.

They bounced into the leaves and pebbles under the grove of trees behind the shuttered concession stand. If I spied it right off, I'd hide it in a paper cup in the fork of a tree or under a trash dumpster, look around a bit more, then walk out with my palms up as if I couldn't find it. Teams would usually send a player to look around, but he was unlikely to discover my hidden treasure.

I retrieved my fair share, however, and liked to show them I could throw, too, firing it over the backstop in a high arc to the waiting catcher, who held out his glove in one hand and mask in the other, hitting the mitt without making him move. These were treasured leather Rawlings game balls, quite often brand new, not like the slippery synthetic-covered ones we played with.

If Granny brought me when Homer was at work at Muskogee Overhead Door, I knew they'd be on time to pick me up around six. But if it was a Saturday and they went "riding around" in the country after they dropped me off, I could be waiting hours if the game ended early due to a run rule or rain. I'd stand on the top row of bleachers and look up and down Shawnee, trying to see the blue pickup.

When it rattled down the gravel driveway leading to the field, I'd run around collecting all the baseballs I'd hidden, sometimes getting into the truck with four or five. Homer showed me how to clean them with bleach and a toothbrush, setting them in the sun on top of the fence poles to dry until shiny white with bright red stitches like right out of the box.

I also spent hours alone watching movies at Muskogee Twin Cinema at Curt's Mall. They'd drop me off in time for the Saturday matinee.

I'd try to watch both movies on one ticket, slipping into the other theater after the first movie ended. When the movies were good you left the air-conditioned coolness in a daze thinking you were still in a New York City apartment in *The Goodbye Girl*, hearing taxicabs honk on rainy streets.

I'd wait outside in the heat for the blue pickup as the employees left and the black asphalt lot emptied of cars. At home I'd lie in bed at night under the fan listening to the little GE clock radio. The song from the movie would come on again with the tinkling of piano and I'd get a lonely feeling of far-off cities and rain and permanent separation, not reunion like the song says.

CHAPTER 13

MY GREAT-AUNT BRENDA'S husband, Harry, dubbed Granny and Homer's place "Little House on the Prairie" after the popular TV show. It was just inside the Muskogee city limits on a hill off a dirt road. Our rural route mailbox was on Harris Road about a half mile to the north, and sometimes we'd find it and others crushed by drunks or delinquents with a ball bat.

Homer, a carpenter, would take it off its post and take it home and hammer it out and repaint it, only to find it bashed in again a few months later. He solved this by making one out of a solid steel tube and attaching a lid and the red flag we raised when we had outgoing mail.

The property was locked from the road by a tall, wide aluminum gate. It was my job to jump out of the truck, undo the simple chain-link hook, swing the gate open, then rehook it, and jump into the bed of the pickup for the curvy, bouncy ride to the house on the hill. It was something I could do in my sleep.

Homer built a fence around it to keep out the cows, using oak poles for posts, leaving the bark on. The yard this created left room for a big garden, twenty rows wide and about fifteen yards long. Each spring Homer spent days tilling the ground, planting cantaloupes, jalapeños, bell peppers, okra, peas, beets, green beans, and squash. Sometimes he'd let me run the big two-handled tiller that you fired up like a lawnmower, but it would jerk me around and take off running like a wild animal.

I'd roll over a ripe watermelon or pluck a fat cucumber only to find holes in them eaten out by turtles. Granny canned vegetables with her big silver canner on the stove with a pressure gauge on top I always thought would explode, using the Kerr or Mason jars that pinged as they cooled, sealing the contents. Homer sometimes sold sacksful of tomatoes to a burger place by Sadler Junior High, but mainly we ate them, canned them, or gave them away.

I developed a taste for fried green tomatoes and fried okra and squash with the golden-brown flour coating or I carried a shaker of salt to the garden and ate tomatoes right off the vine. Crunchy radishes were good, too, with the salt. Now, vegetables from the store are tasteless to me and fruit like peaches are bland and dry compared to the juicy sweet ones from orchards in Porter that Granny brought home.

The corn section was like its own little forest with the dry bronze tassels, taller than I was, shaking in the breeze. Homer would wake me up sometimes while it was still dark to go fishing. He would have a fire going in the woodstove and eggs and bacon ready on the table. While I ate he sharpened our hooks with a small file, slowly rasping them to a fine point, testing them with a fingertip, holding them up to the light.

Before we went to the Arkansas River we went into the garden in darkness and Homer aimed his flashlight around on the cornstalks

Around 1977, at age eleven, with Homer at the kitchen table in Muskogee. Homer, around age fifty here, was a carpenter, fisherman, gardener, and TV sports fanatic. Originally from Blocker, Oklahoma, in Pittsburg County, he's buried at Fort Gibson National Cemetery in Fort Gibson, Oklahoma. (Courtesy of the author.)

and leaves, glittering with dew. Sometimes an owl in the big tree in the corner hooted out eight notes that sounded like, *"What's up with you? What's up with youuuuu?"* When we saw a grasshopper, Homer shined the light in its eyes, blinding it, and I could pick it off like picking a berry. I'd feel it nibble, kicking its yellow tiger-striped legs, and watch it spit "tobacco juice" on my finger. Sometimes it leapt off before I could poke it into the pop bottle, but Homer never got mad.

At daybreak we drove down Harris Road past the spot where Granny always said she saw a bear once, and across the narrow Arkansas River bridge near Bacone College. Sometimes a train blew by so close on the adjacent tracks it looked like you could reach out and touch it. Homer parked off the side of the road and we climbed down with our throw lines—a trotline cut into sections containing four or five big hooks.

We went to a bend in the river and baited with the fat yellow hoppers or chunks of beef liver. After staking one end in the ground or knotting it on a limb, he tied a chunk of brick on the other end and whirled the whole line at an angle into the current, which dragged the cord straight. We did this every ten yards or so until we had four or five lines set.

We returned in the evening or the following morning. I was always excited to see what we had caught. Sometimes the milky brown water had risen and covered our lines and we had to come back the next day. If the line was taut or the limb jerking, then you had caught something, hopefully not a turtle.

You pulled it in with your hands, dragging big catfish onto the bank. I once caught a snake and jumped back, dropping the line, but Homer hauled it in and said it was just an eel, and let it go. Other eccentric catches were spoonbills—a scaleless creature with a long paddlelike beak—and alligator gar, which have long snouts with rows of sharp teeth.

CHAPTER 14

GRANNY AND HOMER each had their respective rural backgrounds, but not necessarily in farming or ranching. We only had to notify Homer's brother George if a cow had gotten loose from the surrounding acreage, which meant driving to the 12th and Broadway phone booth. Lonnie and I flattened the barbed wire on the surrounding fences with our feet and stretched the one above to allow ourselves through while hunting or fishing. The wire was spotted with tufts of black and blond cattle hair, caught when cows stuck their heads through the fence to eat on the other, greener side.

We didn't have to feed or otherwise care for the docile animals. I'd plunk at them with my BB gun while they licked the pink salt blocks, the copper beads bouncing off their hides harmlessly. After someone left the gate to the yard open, Granny and Homer awoke to a cow sticking its head through the curtains on their bedroom window, which had been left open for the breeze on a summer night. It made for a good laugh until Homer went out in the yard with his coffee and found them trampling the garden, one with a window screen frame hanging around its neck.

One afternoon Homer was cutting wood with his chainsaw in another field across the road as a blizzard approached, trying to get us stacked up before the storm. He got his truck stuck in mud and had to walk home, carrying his saw. He cut the tops off a few of the fence posts for our firewood that night. The snow and ice had socked in the whole town and knocked out electricity, but we had the woodstove and a Coleman lantern, which we normally only used for night fishing.

Homer tried smoking coffee grounds for his cigarettes and nearly choked coughing every time he inhaled. I couldn't go without the Sunday *Muskogee Phoenix*, however, and Granny gave me two quarters the next morning and I walked about a mile one-way to get the paper from Arnold's Fruit on Shawnee Bypass.

That was when you didn't know all the college football outcomes until you saw them in the paper. The *Phoenix* ran scores from the big games in big type on a banner at the top of the front page. The next day the ground had frozen hard enough for Homer to drive the truck out of the mudhole and into town for a can of PA.

We saved all our aluminum cans in a circular pen outside that Homer made from chicken wire that stood as tall as I did. When it was full, he'd smash the cans on a stump with the broadside of a hammer, sitting in a chair in the yard. He stood one on end and put pressure on it with his leather work boot.

"Reach down there and flick it with your finger like this, Hoss," he told me.

It pancaked instantly under his boot. But that was just a trick: Homer methodically flattened cans with the hammer and I'd stomp them wearing my baseball cleats. It grew hot and sweat dripped off the end of his nose. When we were all done, we scooped them into big plastic trash bags and loaded them in the bed of the pickup, along with our propane tank to be refilled, and drove across town to Yaffe Iron and Metal on South G Street near the fairgrounds. Yaffe sponsored the Scrappers, one of the teams in my league.

Flattened vehicles rose in towers surrounded by mounds of shiny aluminum that glared in the sun. Piles of rusting iron were heaped beside the railroad tracks while yellow machines with big claws crunched and ripped metal, swiveling them onto mangled stacks.

Homer told an attendant we had aluminum and drove onto a slab next to the weigh station. A worker ran a magnet on the end of a shaft like a golf club over the load, checking for steel or metal, then went into his hut and scribbled on a pad and motioned us on. We drove off and unloaded all the cans onto a big pile. Sometimes the bags dripped with sour-smelling beer and sticky leftover pop. Then we drove back onto the slab to weigh again, and the worker came out with a receipt, which Homer cashed in the office.

If we had a small load, we took it to the Golden Goat on Main and Shawnee next to the auto parts store. You dumped the cans into a chute on the side, hit a button, and it sucked them in, rejecting steel or metal. The cans clattered until the machine silenced with a hum and spit out change, including Susan B. Anthony dollars.

There was an Arby's across the street and we'd drive through, getting an order for Granny, too, and head home. I couldn't wait and ate mine on the way. Homer's favorite was the little foil-wrapped sandwiches of Classic Roast Beef, no sauce. It's the only fast food I ever saw him eat.

*　　*　　*

Homer was the most honest person I ever knew. He'd take change back into stores after he reviewed a receipt and found he'd been returned too much, even if it was just a few cents. One day I watched him argue over money with his brother-in-law John Lowrimore in John's front yard in Muskogee under the shade trees. John, who worked at Cole Grain, always wore denim overalls flecked with sweet-smelling feed dust. Brass hooks connected the straps over his shoulders.

If we met him at work, he'd take me into the steel-cage elevators in the spacious warehouse and let me ride up and down with him. Dust sprinkled through the air in beams of light and golden nuggets of dried corn slid by on automated troughs. It was very loud and you had to yell. He'd rummage in his pockets and produce two quarters for me, working the tobacco in his jaw as we rode the elevator.

In the yard, John folded up a twenty-dollar bill and stuffed it in Homer's shirt pocket. Homer was painting his house but wasn't finished yet.

"Now, John, that's too much. We don't need that much," Homer said, and put the twenty back into the front pocket on John's overalls.

John shook his head, spat, and put it back in Homer's pocket. Homer took it out and put it back in John's pocket. They did this back and forth several more times until I shot Homer in the butt with my BB gun.

Homer yelped, grabbing at his rear.

"What'd you do that for, Hoss?"

I didn't have an explanation. I just felt like shooting him; I didn't think it would hurt. But it must have stung, the way he leaped and yelled, the BB bouncing off his pocket like it did off the cows. His sister Juanita would visit on North 17th Street and they'd do the same routine when she was leaving. We probably needed the money, but it was an old country tradition where you tried to give it back several times before accepting. Like standing on the porch and waving when your visitors were leaving until they couldn't see you anymore.

CHAPTER 15

ALWAYS ON THE hunt for bargains, we collected S&H Green Stamps. According to how many groceries you bought, cashiers revolved a circular dial on a machine that looked like an old rotary phone and a line of pale green and perforated postage-like stamps snaked out the bottom. Really big purchases resulted in a long, curling roll you collected and traded in for merchandise at the S&H store.

My favorite cashier rang up items quickly without even looking at the register. With her left hand she sorted through items from the cart and passed them on to the sacker while her other hand punched buttons, fingers flying around the numbered keys. I always wondered how she could do that with her eyes focused on the price tags. She'd ask if we collected stamps, then dialed the machine.

I had a catalogue that showed what you could buy with the stamps, which I kept in a Folger's coffee can before transferring them into "books." I licked the gummed backs and stuck them onto squares in the pamphlets. One hundred books got you a new charcoal grill, deck furniture, or luggage set. I had my eye on a rod-and-reel combination, which commanded only twenty books. I already had a Zebco 33, but this reel looked nothing like it with its exposed line encircled by a big silver ring.

I'd seen pro fishermen like Jimmy Houston, Roland Martin, and Bill Dance use these reels from their boats on Saturday morning TV. "Son!" they'd say, hooking a big bass as their rod tips bent in a severe curve. "That's what it's all about right there," Houston said to the camera, holding the fish by its gaping jaws, kissing it, and letting it go! I was always astounded when they tossed their catch back into the water. We usually cooked and ate ours the same day. I never saw them use a Zebco 33, so these reels had to be the answer to the lunkers we sought at Taft Lake.

I had become a member of the Bass Anglers Sportsman Society and, with a yearly subscription to its magazine, received a package of Mepps lures, plastic worms, and a Rapala fillet knife with a leather sheath and pocket sharpener. I stuck a B.A.S.S. decal on the back window of the truck showing a bass leaping from the water with its mouth wide open. I knew I could catch bigger ones with the reel I saw in the catalogue.

I rummaged through Granny's purse, where there were always stray stamps, or searched the glove box of the pickup, pawed through dresser drawers. Sometimes you'd find them flying around in the parking lot at the store. It was a long and arduous process for a kid like me with no patience. Sometimes it took a month just to fill one book and I'd try to forget about it; then when the can began to fill or Granny came back with a long strip after a grocery run, I'd start counting and sticking the stamps in books and scanning the catalogue again.

I got the books from my drawer and recounted them. I had it calculated down to the last few stamps. I brought the books when

Granny drove to the store and when she came out I licked in the final row of five in the truck. I now had twenty books. The S&H store was in the same strip on Broadway and 12th and we walked over.

My eyes were instantly drawn to the baseball gloves in the sporting goods section, but they were all plastic, I could tell right away. The reel lay under a glass case in a tall package with the two-piece rod section. I handed the clerk the twenty books, all puffed up with stamps instead of flat and empty. I couldn't wait to show Homer.

He put the unit together, fastening the reel, joining the rods, and running the line through the guides, attaching a swivel, split shot lead, golden Eagle Claw hook, and red-and-white bobber above it all. Taking dirt backroads instead of the highway, we headed for the lake, passing a farmhouse with a hand-painted sign touting EGGS FER SALE, and stopped at a country store near Taft for "minners," as Homer called them, which darted in gurgling tanks in back, dark-green bullet-shaped shadows. We usually got a dozen large and a couple of dozen medium for our bucket, but no matter which combination we chose it seemed we always ran out of the size the fish were biting.

We were never in a rush to get there, which only increased my anticipation, stopping at Granny's favorite shady horse apple tree after the bait shop for a snack and something to drink out of the ice chest. A family in a truck with kids in back slowly passed, everyone waving. We waved back. Everyone always waved in the country.

From there, I could see for miles all around. Weather-beaten gray barn off to the right, but no house. Old wooden windmill to the left. Two scissortails, tail feathers like slender, swooping peace signs, lighted on a high-line wire. On top of a telephone pole sat bell-shaped, lens-blue glass insulators that Granny collected and cleaned and placed on the kitchen windowsill when she found one on the ground. I picked up a fat parrot-green horse apple and felt its heft, getting a little of the white sticky glue on my fingers.

I fired it at the birds for the fun of it, just to watch them fly. They soared off together, violet underbellies flashing. Across the field, haze shimmered off scorched grass, and winged grasshoppers flew near a pond, which was motionless except for the occasional concentric rings created by fish fanning their tail fins just under the surface or rising to snatch a dragonfly.

The pond looked serene but was likely full of copperheads and cottonmouths, baby bullheads and bluegill, surly snapping turtles. Skinny white cattle birds stood stork-like in the shallows, plunging their heads in. I heard the buzz of locusts and crackling sounds like cellophane unraveling. It sounded like the earth was frying. Diamondbacks, chiggers, ticks, scorpions, centipedes, fiddleback spiders: I knew what lived underneath this layer of serenity.

A quail twice tweeted the sharp two notes that had given it its name: *"Bob White? . . . Bob White?"* it seemed to ask. It pierced the static with startling clarity, snapping me from my reverie. I scanned the field looking for it, but it was a bird often heard yet seldom seen.

When we got back in the truck, I asked Homer if we were going to catch anything.

"We're going to catch us some BIIIIIIGGGGG-uns today, Hoss," he said, drawing it out and speaking real deep at the end. Which is what he said every time I asked.

The lake was hidden from the state highway by a grassy ridge. You could only see a sliver of it if you knew when and where to look. Because motorized boating and swimming weren't allowed, it was overlooked by anglers who traveled to big reservoirs like Eufaula, Fort Gibson, Tenkiller, Greenleaf, or Keystone in Tulsa.

The turnoff was a small gravel road with a cattle guard marked by a tiny sign, TAFT LAKE. The truck bounced up the steep hill, minnow bucket and ice chest sloshing, jacks and chains making a racket in back. At the top of the rise the lake spread open before us. I always looked across the shimmering blue to see if anyone had claimed our favorite spot on the bank under a big tree. No one had.

But what started out as a promising trip soon turned sour. My first problem was the bulky new reel was upside down. With the Zebco, the reel was faceup as you cast out. The second problem was it was left-handed. The handle was on the left, unlike the 33, which was on the right. I was right-handed, after all. Homer cast in with one of the big minnows, tossing it far out in a towering arc. He squatted and began to roll a cigarette, sprinkling the brown shreds from the Prince Albert can, eyes darting back and forth to the water. His bobber started jumping and disappeared as he tried to roll and lick his paper. He sprang up to grab his pole, kicked over his can of beer, dropped his tobacco, missed the fish, and lost his bait all in one graceful act.

I hooked a minnow near its tail, wound up, and let it fly. The line whizzed out but jerked abruptly and the minnow went sailing through the air alone into the water like an acrobat. I looked at the reel like it was a great foreign mystery. I never had a problem with my Zebco, which had a silver cone-shaped cover.

"Here, Stud," Homer said, taking the rod. "It's like this here."

He folded back the silver bail, which clicked, and cradled the line with his index finger.

"It's all in the wrist," he said, puffing a cigarette with the rod over his shoulder.

He cast and the line went straight up into the tree. Granny couldn't help herself and laughed from the truck, where she was listening to music on the radio. Homer tried to jerk it all down, but it was hopelessly tangled, bobber stuck in the branches. He bit the line off and rerigged it. I baited another hook and he showed me again how to flip the bail and cradle the line. I walked away from the tree and threw it in.

I didn't like reeling it left-handed and upside down and hassling with the bail and the line, so I got my 33 out of the truck. We caught a few. Homer won five to three. I helped him clean the bass in bowls under the porch light at home, gutting, cutting off heads and tails, and scraping scales.

Homer never filleted them; he was expert at eating around the bones. Granny fried them coated with cornmeal in the cast-iron skillet. The fancy reel was relegated to a back room where it lay in a bird's nest of line for months until I gave it to Lonnie.

After we had stopped at the grocery store for cornmeal and eggs returning from the lake, I already had a few more Green Stamps collected in the can and started thumbing through the catalogue again that night. I saw a pellet gun. *Air rifle* was the description. Thirty books. It had to be better than my Daisy BB gun, I thought.

CHAPTER 16

FOOTBALL WAS A big thing at the Little House on the Prairie, especially University of Oklahoma football, which dominated in the 1970s. We had a nineteen-inch black-and-white TV connected to a tall antenna anchored in the ground on the side of the house that picked up three Tulsa stations: Channel 8 (ABC), Channel 6 (CBS), and Channel 2 (NBC). If the reception was fuzzy, we'd go out and wrestle the antenna pole. Inside, others would yell, "little bit more!" or "back a little!" or "right there!" when the picture quit flipping and sharpened into focus.

The biggest thrill when OU ran its wishbone offense was when the quarterback, usually a tiny jitterbug against the hulking linebackers and linemen, ran the option to the corner and got creamed by a blitzing cornerback.

Just as he was getting flattened to the ground he'd pitch the ball to a halfback on his right, who'd catch it sprinting at full speed and streak down the field right in front of his teammates on the sideline who jumped and yelled, holding their helmets in the air in front of a sea of screaming crimson-clad fans.

Sometimes we turned down the TV and listened on the radio.

"Elvis Peacock's at the 30, 35-40," John Brooks announced, voice rising with each word. "Forty-five–50, 45-40! Gets a block!

Thirty-five–30, 25–20, 15, 10, 5—touchdown, Oklahoma! Jiiiiiiiiiiminy, Christmas!"

I never saw Granny so animated as during the Orange Bowl, leaping up from the couch and screaming, "Go, go, go!" Of course, I yelled as well. Homer was on the edge of his seat, too, stomping the floor, slapping himself all around because in the excitement he'd forgotten to flick his Prince Albert in the ashtray and sparks flew across his arms and down his chest, burning holes in his shirt. His shirts and pants always had little burn holes in them. It's a wonder he never set his chair afire.

Living in the country had other dangers besides fire. There was the leader of the cattle herd: a big, shiny brown "Bremer" bull with a hump on its back. But he hardly came near the house it seemed, staying in the far eastern stretch of pasture. He only got agitated when we came around him on purpose, seeking him out to see if he'd chase us, clapping and yelling around his periphery just for the excitement. Granny would have been exasperated if she knew we were doing that. A couple of times he made a bluffing charge, snorting and roaring a bellowing howl, which was enough to scare us away.

There were chiggers, thorns of various sorts from blackberry bushes, stickers and burrs that stuck to your socks and shoelaces and took forever to disengage. There were angry little black mosquitoes that left welts on your arms and face. Coveys of camouflaged quail erupted in front of you, flushing from the ground in a thunderous explosion, shocking you from daydreams and making your heart skip.

There were scorpions, bees, wasps (which I called "waspers"), and yellowjackets, which built dirt hives on the roof of our porch and flew into the house when the screen door opened. "Dirt daubers," as we called them, were a shiny blue-black with a long, sharp stinger.

Other spongelike structures with octagonal holes would sprout under the eaves of the house and Homer would light newspaper on fire and smoke the hornets out and torch the nests because Dawn was allergic to bee or wasper stings. If she was stung anywhere on her body, her entire face puffed up until her eyes nearly shut. Or she'd step into poison oak or ivy and Granny would slather her whole body in calamine lotion, where it dried like a pale pink second skin.

Oklahoma has seven species of venomous snakes: cottonmouths, copperheads, and five kinds of rattlers, many of which are native to our area. Homer's childhood friend Gene Lemmons, from Blocker, Oklahoma, visited one day and I went walking with them in the fields, down into the little canyons where people dumped trash.

Gene had just one arm. I was staring at the shirtsleeve he had pinned up to his shoulder when he dropped to the ground. I thought he had stepped in a gopher hole, another hazard of walking around in the pasture. In a flash he whipped out a pocketknife and cut the head off a snake, which he had pinned to the ground with his knee.

"Copperhead," he announced, standing up and dusting himself off.

Homer and I looked on stunned; we never even saw the snake, which despite its name, can be dust-colored and blend in among grass and leaves. Outside of that, I rarely saw snakes. Sometimes I'd see one sliding in curves across the pond or on roads run over by a car. But they weren't something we walked around in fear of. My cousin Joe and I saw one in a tree while walking to the convenience store on Harris and Highway 69 and pelted it with rocks until it was just a pile of meat. I often wondered why we did that. It wasn't threatening us or posing any harm up in the branches off the side of the road.

There were dangerous spiders, too, the black widow and the brown recluse, called fiddleback because of the violin-shaped marking on its exterior. At his house one summer morning Lonnie threw on his T-shirt, which had been lying on the floor, and was bitten by one under his armpit. It only stung at first, he said, then as the day wore on, it heated up like fire. It put him in the hospital, eventually rotting out flesh. He had to miss the rest of our baseball season, but he still showed up to practices and games wearing a white sling.

Then there were ticks. A small pooch arrived at our porch whining, blotted with wrinkly gray blobs that covered his back and belly. I pinched one and blood spurted out. Homer tried everything on him: Sevin insect garden dust, Coleman lantern fuel, gasoline, and finally bathed him in Pennzoil 30-weight, which seemed to do the trick.

A few days of this treatment eradicated the bloodsuckers and we bought him a collar and I named him Bozo, a term my uncle Jackson always used. The German shepherd-looking canine became my companion, walking with me to check the mail, fishing at the ponds, where he'd bark at the croaking bullhead catfish I caught, or chasing down baseballs I'd crack high into the air off my wooden bat. I could never get him to bring them back, though.

*   *   *

When Dawn was around six she fell ill, running a fever. She didn't recover after a few days so she was taken to the Indian clinic in nearby Tahlequah, capital of the Cherokee Nation. Under a treaty with the United States government, Native Americans are guaranteed free medical care at these Indian Health Service hospitals or tribal clinics.

Doctors there couldn't determine what was wrong with her other than a fever so they sent her home with aspirin. Granny had already been giving her aspirin and it wasn't working, as Dawn's symptoms grew to include headache, body ache, and chills. After a few days, Momma and Granny took her to the Children's Hospital in the capital, Oklahoma City, about two hours west.

She was admitted immediately, and her condition worsened. Hallucinating in her bed, her fever reached 103, and she was in constant pain. She was parched but not allowed liquids, so Granny fed her ice, which she crunched and sucked on, her eyes vacant, her face puffy.

A battery of tests revealed days later, after a long process of elimination, that she had contracted Rocky Mountain spotted fever. Relatives visited and one great-uncle, Jacob, who was a Baptist preacher, stood over her bed and prayed, both in English and Creek. She improved after a series of antibiotics and was discharged after a week. Doctors later said she had been near death.

The disease is unpredictable, almost impossible to diagnose immediately because the symptoms are associated with a wide range of maladies, and can be devastating for the very young and very old. Granny took it hard, blamed herself because she hadn't checked Dawn for ticks after she came in from playing in the yard. But you can't expect someone to do that on an hourly basis when your playground is a pasture or field in the country. She was more likely to get bitten by a rattlesnake or struck by lightning than catch tick fever.

CHAPTER 17

AFTER DAWN RECOVERED, I started sixth grade. Sounds simple enough, but I wound up going to five schools that year. I enrolled at Harris-Jobe in Muskogee only to discover after one day that it was the wrong school due to a mix-up over busing routes. I transferred to Riverside, leaving there after Roman got a new job in Pampa, Texas, driving a semitrailer truck for the oil fields. The plan was for my sisters and brother to join us when we got settled. For now, Dawn remained with Granny and Homer while Anthony and Missy were staying at Grandpa and Grandma Green's in Calera.

We packed the Pontiac Catalina full of clothes, dishes, lamps, and our cat, Jimmy, and Momma followed Roman and me for the six-hour trip west along Interstate 40. I wanted to ride with Roman because I'd never been in an eighteen-wheeler and showed this by scorching my leg on a hot steel exhaust pipe climbing into my seat.

Crossing into the Texas Panhandle, the land became treeless and flat, and outside of Amarillo we rolled up our windows against the smell of cattle slaughterhouses. We checked into a hotel room provided by Roman's company, which gave us a month to look for a house. The next morning Momma enrolled me at Pampa Junior High, producing my birth certificate, vaccination records, and addresses and phone numbers of my schools in Muskogee. It was after lunch when a principal finally walked me down the hallway to my first class.

"So, Mr. Eddie, how long do you think you'll be here in Pampa?" she said.

"A long time," I said, having no reason to think otherwise. "We'll probably be here a long time."

We entered the room in the middle of geography hour, and I was introduced to the teacher, who welcomed me and assigned me a seat near the back of the room. The walls were covered with maps and a fat world globe sat on her desk. I figured I'd just sit silently for the remainder of the period, then focus on making it to my next class, when everyone stood abruptly and belted out a song—led by the teacher conducting behind her stand—apparently a time-honored ritual for new students.

"Pampa Junior High is best! Green and gold outshines the rest!" they sang loudly, all standing and facing me. "Reapers loyal, brave, and strong! Victory is our song! With Pampa honor, class, and pride, winning is our way of life! Reapers we will be true blue! Green and gold, we love you!"

At "you" my new classmates took their hands off their hearts and pointed at me dramatically. I didn't know what to do so I just sat there with a grin on my face. Just as abruptly as it began, the class sat after a round of applause and the ordeal was over.

I made it through my three remaining classes without such histrionics. At the three o'clock bell I went out front to look for Momma and jogged over to her car in the circular pickup lane carrying an armful of new books and papers, which I couldn't wait to dig into. The Pontiac was packed again to the roof in back with all our stuff.

"We're going back to Muskogee," Momma said when she saw me staring at the loaded-down interior. "We got into it," she said, anticipating my question. "Get in and shut the door."

Noticing Momma's attitude, I knew not to quiz her about what happened. I could always ask Granny after things simmered down. If I had it pegged right, I'd go back to Muskogee, Momma and Roman would get back together, and we'd move again. Sometimes she asked me where I wanted to go to school or if I wanted to live with Granny and Homer, but this time there was no debate.

I can't say I'd grown attached to the school in three hours. At least there'd be no dread in leaving best friends or teammates. I know I told the principal we'd be here a long time, but I must have known it wouldn't be forever. If Roman's job had moved him there so suddenly, it could just as easily move him again. Was I doomed to follow Roman around the country?

We pulled out of the driveway in line with a bunch of other cars and I looked back at the squat, brick building, knowing it would be the last time I'd see it. I could forget all the new names I'd been memorizing, including the school lyrics they gave me to learn for the next new kid. As we went down I-40 I pictured the teacher calling out my name in the morning and everyone turning to see the empty desk. Pampa, I hardly even knew you.

I was right. I eventually landed at Webster Middle School in Oklahoma City, where I was forced into a wrestling singlet for the first time. I was baseball, football, and basketball—not wrestling. The way I viewed it was if I wanted to wrestle, I would have joined wrestling. But at Webster, it was part of PE and we slipped into the skintight uniform in the middle of the day. I thought, *We didn't have to do this at Muskogee*, staring at the point my weenie made in the crotch of my tights. I don't remember actually wrestling much in the hour-long class; most of the time was spent running around the gym or climbing a thick, knotted rope hanging from the rafters that burnt my hands when I slid too fast coming down. But at least at Webster I eclipsed the one day and three-hour time spans for attendance.

Somehow the English teacher figured out I liked books and had me start off reading aloud from mimeographed pages of John Steinbeck's *The Red Pony*, the light-blue ink still smelling fresh. Here was my chance to show off for the new teacher, display my skills as the new kid again. I started out evenly, not stumbling over words or stuttering or running through sentences, honoring the comma breaks and periods with just the right pauses, hitting a rhythm:

> *At daybreak Billy Buck emerged from the bunkhouse and stood for a moment on the porch looking up at the sky. He was a broad, bandy-legged little man with a walrus mustache, with square hands, puffed and muscled on the palms.*

I continued in a confident, steady voice, not rushing, enunciating at the right times. If I'd had a glass of water I would have held up a respectful finger and taken a quick gulp like a professional speaker at a lectern. Then the teacher said keep reading and just left the room. I glanced up—she was actually leaving—lost my place for a second, but recovered and read on as she left and closed the door. I went on for a page until some model-like blond blue-eyed kid with a tan and feathered hair started coughing, drowning me out.

I had to raise my voice over it, then he did it again, putting his fist to his mouth and coughing dramatically louder, drawing a few kids into giggles. I actually sort of grinned along in acknowledgment—hey, I can take a joke—but kept reading through it, raising my voice but not losing my place or my composure. He coughed; I kept reading. I wasn't going to stop. This went on until the teacher came back and he quit amid general chuckling from the class. On the way out of the room I eyeballed him, but he wouldn't look at me. Probably couldn't read anyway.

We lived at 6306 Anderson Drive in the Valley Brook section of south Oklahoma City. We started out with nothing again. I didn't have a bike or a skateboard. We had no TV or stereo. But we had a telephone, and I had a transistor radio and became obsessed with calling in to station KOMA-AM 1520, which played rock and pop favorites. I'd almost miss the school bus trying to be the fifteenth caller in the morning.

After weeks of dialing, I got through, winning the Jimmy Buffett record *Changes in Latitudes, Changes in Attitudes*, which had "Margaritaville" as a big hit the station played a lot. Momma drove me to the studios about ten minutes away in Moore in Roman's work truck to collect my album, which I took out and looked at a lot, wondering, *What are changes in latitudes and attitudes?* If the answer was contained in the songs, I never heard it because we didn't have a record player.

The Sooners had a big game at Ohio State, which we listened to on the radio. Roman was out of town, working. The game came down to the final seconds, with Oklahoma kicker Uwe von Schamann leading fans in chants of "Block that kick! Block that kick!" like an orchestra conductor after Ohio State coach Woody Hayes called time out.

After he made the field goal for the win, I ran into the backyard screaming and jumping around like a madman. Later, Momma gave me a few dollars to go to the store a few blocks away for baloney, bread, chips, and pop. We were still waiting for Roman to get back from work with his paycheck as we had plans to go out to eat.

At the store, I noticed Roman's white company pickup across the street. It was unmistakably his, with a pair of long, whiplike antennas on each side.

"I saw Roman's truck," I said when I returned, aiming my voice down the hallway.

"Really? Where?" Momma said, leaning out of the bedroom. She probably thought I had seen a similar vehicle on the road because Roman was out of town.

"At that bar across the street from the store." I said it matter-of-factly, but I knew this was likely to ignite a firestorm.

She came out with her purse and her grim no-messing-around expression.

"I'll be right back."

I ate a sandwich at the kitchen table while she went to investigate. Should I have said anything? I was sure it was his truck, and, after all, we were waiting on him. Turned out I was right.

After she came back, I discerned from the shouting in the bedroom there had been quite a scene at the "gentlemen's establishment," which were the words I later saw from the school bus on a sign outside the place. Well, Roman was a gentleman, wasn't he?

By now I had grown accustomed to changing schools and towns. Usually, I never knew it was coming, but this time I could sense it. I thought moving so much was normal. I also thought everyone lived with their grandparents, too, at least some of the time.

I stood with the only real friend I'd made in my short time at Webster after school that Monday. We were talking about the big OU win while I waited on a bus, and he waited on his parents. I said it was good meeting him. And I meant it. We could talk about books and sports, and he played baseball, too.

"But I don't think I'm ever going to see you again," I told him. He laughed at first, then looked at me strange, and ran off to his mom's car. It was true; we moved, and I never saw him after that.

That was always happening. I made friends easily enough at school and would sometimes spend the night at their house and vice versa. But when we moved it was a complete split: no writing letters back and forth, no phone calls, certainly no out-of-town visits.

And the moves didn't necessarily come after the school year. It could be midweek. Friends vanished and became replaced by new names, other faces, different personalities. Only Lonnie, whose mom was a teacher, remained some sort of fixture because he never moved from the same house down from Granny and Homer's and we played on the same baseball team every year.

CHAPTER 18

WE WERE ALL split up once again. I never knew how these Momma-Roman separations would leave our living situations, but, as usual, I wound up back at the reliable standby: Granny and Homer's in Muskogee. Missy and Anthony went back to Grandma and Grandpa Green's in Calera while Dawn stayed with Momma in town. I assumed this was temporary and that we'd be reunited again; with time we usually were. But gradually, being split up became the norm instead of the exception.

I missed Anthony, six years younger, following me around all the time and asking questions. At only seven or eight years old, he could play catch with me and hit me grounders. He was also surprisingly good at basketball, where he had to launch his whole body into the air to make a shot.

I went through a cruel period, though, when he was younger and learning to talk. I pointed to a radio.

"What's that?" I said.

"Radio."

"No, it's a TV. What's that?" I said, pointing at the TV.

"TV."

"No, it's a radio."

With my brother, Anthony (left), and sister Missy, Christmastime circa 1977 at Granny and Homer's on North 17th Street in rural Muskogee. Oftentimes the tree would be decorated with acorn shells and silver-and-red tin strips from Homer's Prince Albert tobacco cans. (Courtesy of the author.)

"No it's not," he said.

I also tried to convince him that the replica Statue of Liberty in a pond at Spaulding Park in Muskogee was the real deal, but by then he was too old for that.

I missed periods of school during these moves and family shake-ups, but never enough to affect my grades, it seemed. Sometimes I'd enroll in a new school and discover the subjects they were studying I'd covered the year before.

As winter thawed toward spring, I spent one long night getting a science project ready for class at Pershing Elementary in Muskogee, my fifth school in sixth grade and where I was reunited with Lonnie.

It was laid out on the kitchen table, all ready to go, a drawing of a figure in a colonial hat holding a strand of Granny's red yarn with a key dangling from it that I'd taped onto the poster board. Lightning zapped the key from clouds above in a dramatic zigzag pattern. The bold caption I scrawled above his head said, "BENJAMIN FRANKLIN THOUGHT HE WAS COOL, BUT IN ACTUALITY HE WAS REALLY A FOOL!" It was my comprehensive treatise on weather safety.

I got up as soon as the radio alarm went off and got dressed. Granny didn't have to continually wake me this morning.

"Shoo-wee, what's that smell?" I said, sitting down to my customary bacon and eggs.

"Skunk got under the house," Homer said across from me, slurping his coffee. "Guess he got into it with a possum or something. Skunk won from the smell of things."

They let me off at Pershing and I went into homeroom carrying my project, convinced it would win first place. A few other kids gave their presentations before me, standing at the front of the room near the teacher and explaining their projects: diagrams of plants sprouting in various types of soil under different levels of sunlight, mold grown in petri dishes, diagrams of geologic formations and volcanic rocks. Kathy Teafatiller was explaining her photo display of dissected frogs with arrows pointing to key internal organs.

"Holy smokes!" some kid shouted out. "Anybody else smell that? Smells like skunk."

The entire class erupted like someone had pooted, waving their hands, holding their noses. It caused so much commotion, stirring up the scent, that Mrs. Hill led us all outside while custodians searched the room and sprayed it down with air freshener.

Apparently, the skunk aroma leaked between the floorboards and permeated everything in our house in the country on 17th Street, and over the hours we'd grown accustomed to it. In the fresh air outside, I lifted my jacket sleeve to my nose and finally smelled it.

I stuffed the windbreaker into the trash in the bathroom and as the day wore on the smell lessened. But in a crowded basement homeroom with no windows, it must have reeked to "high heaven," as Granny would say. It was a narrow escape. No one ever figured out it was me. I don't know how they would have sent me home anyway; we didn't have a phone.

Toward the end of the year, it was time for baseball tryouts. A year older, I would be in the Midget classification in Knothole, up from Pee Wee A. I had missed the playoffs with the Kiwanis but felt I had a better shot with new players at a different school.

But when I went to the field, a team was already out there taking infield practice. Players were at every position and the coach was hitting them grounders and flies. I stood around on the side with Lonnie and some other players from school: Darrell Horsechief and Dean Cheater, who were Native; a few Black kids, including Tony Tollett and Bobby Gandy; and James Cordero, my Filipino American classmate, whose dad was a doctor at Muskogee General.

"Isn't this the tryouts?" I asked an older kid whose brother was practicing.

"No, they just decided to go with the team they had last year," he said. "They went to the playoffs and they've got everybody back this season."

The coach threw the ball sky-high around home plate for the catcher. After the catcher flung his mask away and caught it, the team came running in. I recognized them as older white kids who hung out together at Pershing. They brushed right through us like we weren't there.

I asked the coach when the tryouts were.

"Hold on here a second—we'll get you guys out there in a minute."

I played catch with Lonnie—we'd both made the All-Star team last summer—while the coach talked with his players. They had taken a knee in front of the backstop.

"All right, you guys," the coach said to us after a few minutes, "get out to your positions."

I trotted out to short, Lonnie went to center. The coach hit us one grounder apiece—I caught mine easy enough and threw to first—and the outfielders one fly each and called us in.

"OK, boys," he said. "I don't know what the mix-up was, but I coached my guys here last year and we've got everybody we need. We don't have any more spots."

I looked at James. He had an astounded look on his face. A couple of guys slammed their gloves on the ground.

"But I'm going to talk to the league tonight and see what I can do," the coach continued. "It looks like you've almost got enough for your own team anyway. Have your parents call in a few days and they should let you know something. Good luck."

With that, he motioned his team back onto the field and continued practice. It was the first time I'd felt totally ignored and excluded from a sport I loved. Sure, the coach had his whole team back from last year and wanted to keep it together, but there was something about the way his players barely even looked at us and didn't talk. Was it because we weren't white? The more I thought about it, I realized they didn't talk much to us at school, either. I wasn't friends with any of them, but that could have been because I was new and they were in a different grade. It was mystifying.

Horsechief and Tollett had brought bats and I had a ball, so we went over to the little softball field in the corner and played around awhile. I heard the coach behind me hitting infield practice and the players yelling and shouting.

I lobbed a few pitches to Gandy, a fifth grader I thought didn't even play baseball. He swung wildly and missed every one.

"Aw, man," Tollett shouted from left field, "you sorry!"

The playoffs weren't looking likely this summer. Some kids started drifting away until only a few of us remained. Lonnie left after his mom drove up.

"You want to walk to my place and get some ice water?" Horsechief asked me.

Granny and Homer were picking me up after "tryouts," but I figured I had enough time.

"Sure. Where's it at?"

"This way," he said.

After a few blocks I followed him into a restaurant on Okmulgee. He went to the counter and asked for two ice waters. A waitress brought them in clear plastic cups, and we began walking back to Pershing.

"I thought we were going to your place," I said.

"We just did. That's My Place. My Place Bar-B-Q."

I realized the tryouts were a sham and that we were unwanted regardless of ability. But there were enough kids wanting to play and a new team was formed, sponsored by City Bank and coached by the Muskogee County district attorney.

"You guys should be called the Little DAs," Homer quipped.

We had brand-new uniforms but were relegated to the small practice field while the all-white team got the big field, which we used when they weren't practicing or had a game at Hatbox. We weren't as good as the other team because we hadn't played together much and were disorganized from the outset. Plus, they were all a year older.

Some guys only came when they wanted, and sometimes we even wondered if the coach was going to show up for practice. Just when we were about to give up on him, he'd roar up in his car and jump out wearing a sports coat, slacks, and dress shoes with a necktie flopped over his shoulder.

"Sorry, boys, got tied up in court," he said.

He was an enthusiastic coach and we liked him, but we just never had any team chemistry. We won a few games, however, but also had to forfeit a few times when not enough players showed.

James Cordero asked me after practice one day if we could pick him up for the game tomorrow. His parents were going out of town, but he didn't want to miss the game. He wrote his address down on a piece of paper. The next day we tried to find his house, circling around, up and down wide, smooth streets in a new addition a few blocks from the school with a confusing bunch of similar-type names.

"Is it Court, Square, Drive, or Lane?" Granny asked. "They all look the same."

The two-story houses had lawns like golf courses and sweeping circular driveways with water fountains and shiny new cars.

"How'd you like to mow one of these, Hoss?" Homer asked.

"Wouldn't," I said.

We finally found the house and I jogged up to the front door, checking the address on the paper. I punched the doorbell and musical chimes cascaded inside.

A Black woman answered the door wearing what looked like a nurse's uniform and hat.

EDDIE CHUCULATE

"Is James here?" I stammered, figuring I had the wrong house.

"James!" she yelled out. "Your ride's here."

James came grinning up to the door in his uniform. We climbed in the bed of the pickup.

On the way to Hatbox, I asked who the woman was.

"That's my mom," he said.

When he saw my look of confusion, he broke out laughing.

"That's our maid, you turkey!"

I chuckled along with him but it still bothered me for a while, even after I got over the fact that she wasn't his mom. He'd said it so matter-of-factly and convincingly I had believed him for a second. And I didn't know people in Muskogee had maids. The only maids I had seen were on *The Brady Bunch* and *The Jeffersons* on TV. Granny cleaned house for a couple of people sometimes but didn't wear any sort of getup. Maybe everyone who had a big house around here also had a maid.

Midway through the season I had to go to Tishomingo in southern Oklahoma where Momma and Roman had gotten back together and I had to miss some games. They had moved into a house and the plan was for me to start seventh grade in Tishomingo in August, but I needed to bring my birth certificate and get vaccinations at a clinic there. I rode the Trailways bus for the first time, alone. We stopped in McAlester and Atoka, and Roman picked me up in Durant. We had a hamburger at a café and he bought me a Louis L'Amour paperback before driving to Tish.

I returned to Muskogee a week later on the same route. Homer picked me up at the Trailways station downtown. When I got back

114

to 17th Street, the first thing I did was check our schedule. It said we had a game the next day at seven at Hatbox 3.

Granny washed and bleached my suit nice and white, and they dropped me off before searching for a parking spot. Games were being played at all the fields, the parking lot was full, and parents and kids filled the complex. There was a game in progress at Hatbox 3, so I looked for my team. Usually, teams that played next were huddled around opposite dugouts waiting, but I saw no one. The game ended and the field cleared.

I asked a woman at the concession stand when game time was at Hatbox 3. She looked at something on the wall and said, "City Bank disbanded. No game at Hatbox 3." I felt stupid walking around in a uniform blaring "City Bank" for a team that didn't exist.

Lonnie and I went fishing for bullheads at the pond across the road a few days later. He told me players quit coming to practice, then games, and after a couple more forfeits the coach called it quits. I figured I had been partly responsible for this dissolution, but there was nothing I could have done. I came back as quick as I could.

"So, you moving to Tishomingo?" Lonnie asked.

"Taking the bus next week."

"You'll come back," he said. "You always do."

I'm third from left, and Lonnie is far right, both front row, ages eleven to twelve, in this Arkhola Sand and Gravel team photo from 1979. Also pictured in front row: far left, Mark Chitwood; and next to him is Kevin Hunter. Middle row: fourth from left, Greg Custer; and fifth from left, Stacey Clark. In the back row, far left, is coach Jimmy Chitwood, and on the far right is assistant Chris James. (Courtesy of Melita Griffith.)

CHAPTER 19

TISHOMINGO, NAMED AFTER a Chickasaw chief, was closer to Roman's stomping grounds and was the historic capital of the Chickasaw Nation, although more white than Indian with just a few Black families, unlike Muskogee. We had a new house in the Chickasaw Nation housing projects: a brick three-bedroom with a carport and backyard, where Roman put up a basketball hoop. We were all together for the first time in years. Dawn and Missy shared a bedroom, as did Anthony and I.

I had a bike and got to know the town quickly, riding it to school, to Larry's IGA, to Mill Pond, to King Theater, over the swinging bridge on Pennington Creek, or to Murray State College, where I watched basketball practice and played the KISS and Evel Knievel pinball machines at the student union.

Except for the times I chose to ride my sunburst-colored GT skateboard down to the IGA to get Momma's Marlboro Light 100s in a box, I was usually on a bike. I got to know all quadrants of town, discovered where the rich folks resided, where the girls I liked from school lived, the shortcut to downtown, the fastest way to my friends' houses, and all the good fishing ponds on the outskirts.

After school I'd wait for the bus to fill and depart, then race it. Shooting through alleys and cutting through yards, darting through traffic, I always beat it home. Sometimes I'd wind up alongside it on the sidewalk and see some of my classmates or my sister Dawn pointing at me and laughing while my windbreaker fanned behind me like a cape.

I wasn't what you'd call a bike freak: buying accessories, riding expensive Mongooses or Treks, bunny hopping, and reading all the magazines. I just had a regular knobby-tired black Huffy and loved to ride it. I liked the way the new tires smelled and was sad to see the whiskers on the tread wear away after a few weeks of riding.

It was my first bike since the one I had gotten in Calera was stolen a year later in Muskogee right off our front porch on South 15th. That flabbergasted me, not understanding when Roman tried to explain that someone had just taken it. I had just learned to ride it without training wheels. I left my bike unlocked everywhere in Tishomingo and it was never stolen.

Like many small towns in Oklahoma, the main highway leading into Tishomingo soon became if not Main Street, then the *main street* with Dairy Queens, convenience stores, flower shops, insurance agencies, funeral homes, hardware stores, and newspaper offices lining both sides of the street on out of town before it became a highway again.

I rode my bike one summer evening to the movies. After Larry's IGA I could coast, the self-generated cooling breeze fluffing my hair. I jostled along the sidewalk that curled around the lumberyard, watching for the black-and-tan German shepherd that barked from inside under the BEWARE OF DOG sign.

Car headlights began to appear in the dusk, but I was on schedule. I passed the intersection that led to my classmate Lisa's house. At our age, "dates" weren't made specific, and not everyone had a telephone. So, when I "happened" to ride by earlier in the week, she and her older sister Angela let drop that they were going to the show Saturday night.

I met my new friend Gary at the theater, racked my bike, and stood in line. Downtown Tish was at its busiest. Teenagers in Camaros or pickups cruised Main, stereos blaring; restaurants were full, and trucks towing boats were returning from the Blue River or Lake Texoma. Twilight was a surreal yellow-orange; streetlamps flickered on, signs at the Lickety Split flashed, and the lights of King Theater's old-fashioned marquee shone down, lacquering us in red. Plain black block letters on the white marquee blared *JAWS*.

I saw Lisa nearing the ticket window for the special showing. She wore a red T-shirt, jean shorts, and little socks with a puff of maroon on the heel above white tennis shoes. She seemed so cool, but not aloof, either. We pretended not to see each other, which was our typical style, full well knowing we would meet there.

"Hey, there goes Lisa," Gary said, slapping me on the ribs.

"I know, I know."

"I think she likes you, man."

Gary was behind the times on that account. He was there to meet Denise Tyson, a tall, slim Chickasaw with long jet-black hair, a girl I loved before Lisa drew my eye: Indian kids pairing off with white classmates, and vice versa.

King Theater was one of the main social gathering points for all ages. Unlike Muskogee, Tish had no bowling alley or roller skating rink—you had to go to Ardmore, Ada, or Durant for that. Friday night home high school football games were another meeting spot.

We played cup ball under the stands in slatted stadium lights and to the drumbeats and trombones of the Pride of Little Dixie marching band, slapping crushed Coke cups with our hands, and sprinting to landmarks such as light poles or rocks for bases. On the field, pads popped, whistles blew, fans yelled, car horns blared.

We also met at Tuesday or Friday night high school basketball games. We congregated at Mill Pond or Pennington Creek, or at Pizza Hut, a block from my house. I'd walk there with a pocketful of quarters and record favorite songs like "My Sharona," "Hot Child in the City," and "Heart of Glass," setting my portable cassette player right next to the jukebox. We also assembled at the café down the hill from the middle school for fifty-cent burritos and eight ball. There wasn't a game room in town, but the café also had Defender and two pinball machines, one with banana flippers. Pizza Hut had Asteroids, and Space Invaders was tucked in a corner at Larry's.

CHAPTER 20

LISA DISAPPEARED INTO the theater, so I cut in line to get my ticket while Gary waited for Denise. The color scheme was red: red upholstered velvet-backed and bottom seats, red neon lights along the walls, and huge red drapes that spread open vertically from the middle at showtime. A pair of industrial-size water coolers rumbled in the rear and aimed their vents right up the two aisles bordering the middle main section.

The breeze whistled in my ear as I scanned for Lisa. I was just in time to see her stepping into the middle rows, glancing back, looking for me, I hoped. The place was as crowded as I'd ever seen. There was giddy anticipation of blood and gore, of limbs being chomped off, sharks getting speared, boats being T-boned by colossal great whites. I sat in the magical vacant seat next to Lisa just as the theater went dark. Her face flickered with previews as I moved my hand onto her leg as was expected from both of us.

She stuck her gum on the lid of her drink to share popcorn with me as the movie started. I looked at her in profile: blond hair feathered on the sides and French braided in back, Roman nose, light from the screen flashing off her face and sparkling her blue eyes. I looked over at Gary and Denise jabbering away, pinching or tickling each other, popping candy in each other's mouths, pointing and giggling. A fin was snaking its way toward a crowd of swimmers, but after all the panic it was only a pair of kids with snorkels and a fake cutout.

Lisa yawned suddenly, arching her back with her hands into fists over her head, and her breasts jutted out, making me blush and look away before she caught me staring. We sat as close together as the armrest would allow. I slipped my arm behind her back, sliding my hand over her taut flesh. The police chief was throwing chum from the stern to set a trap for Jaws.

Lisa yelled when the pale face of the bloated dead boatman—a Jaws victim—flashed suddenly on the screen with the accompanying jolt of sound. I was also startled but tried to hide it in front of Lisa. I munched on Milk Duds and kept my arm around her, as if to protect her from the shark. She surprised me by leaning her head against my shoulder and I brushed the hair back along her temple as we leaned back.

But by the time Jaws attacked the cage and chased its pursuers we were leaning forward in our seats in anticipation. People screamed and clapped at the end when the tank exploded. It was a great movie. We gathered outside, chattering as we walked across the street to Dairy Queen at how big the shark was and how it destroyed the boat. Lisa said she would never go swimming in the ocean. After we ate fries and ice cream Denise's mom picked the girls up. Gary and I rode around on our bikes awhile before also going home. I couldn't wait for our next movie.

*   *   *

I coasted along in school, tops in my class with Gary in English and basic math, above average or average in science, geography, and civics. In woodshop we put screws in the bottoms of legs to balance the coffee tables we built for projects, sanding and staining them. We used mine at home in the living room, adjusting the screws when it got wobbly. In music, during a spelling test on terms and instruments, I blurted out "It can also be bass!" (as in the fish) when the teacher asked us to spell bass (as in the note). I never saw a teacher look so exasperated. He'd warned us about giving away clues to this exact same question prior to the test—I just couldn't help myself.

My only problem at school came in basketball, which was odd because I lived and breathed sports, was an All-Star in summer baseball, shot hoops in our backyard goal year-round 'til midnight, and was a safety, running back, and kickoff returner in football. The problem was Coach Applegate: He terrified me.

He seemed about eighty, not much taller than I was, always wearing a black baseball cap with a white *T* jammed down on his forehead. He wore a whistle, black-framed glasses, and a perpetual scowl like someone had just egged his car. In his red pullover warm-up jacket, he was a yelling machine.

I wasn't accustomed to being screamed at in that fashion, face-to-face. Yelled at by Momma, maybe, but not with spit flying from her mouth, veins popping, and rancid coffee breath. During basketball at two o'clock we were to get dressed in the locker room and get on the bus for a twenty-minute trip to Madill. I didn't want to go to Madill and sit on the bench and watch us lose.

I was hot stuff in the backyard, hitting twenty free throws in a row in the dark, practicing, at five foot one, my sky hook, my finger roll, my over-the-backboard trick shots. But put me on a team with an organized offense and defense and I was lost. Trapping, switching, box and one, triangle and two, weak side help, setting screens, sagging the zone, fighting through picks, crossing over, pivoting, hands! hands! hands! The game was played beyond my hands and above my head. I thought I had no business out there, so I hid from the screaming coach in the locker room.

"Chuculate! Get your butt on the bus!"

I saw him coming. I hid in the toilet, standing on the commode.

"Chuculate! Dang it! If you make us late!"

Patton or MacArthur never barked like this.

He caught me sneaking out the emergency exit.

"Where the heck you going? Bus is out here!"

"I forgot my gym shoes."

"Get your rear on this dang bus!"

I slunk out and got on carrying an almost-empty black gym bag embossed with the official red Tishomingo Indian brave. It was true. I had left my basketball shoes at home. I was in some program that day where we sang a bunch of songs in an all-school assembly, and I had worn my only pair of dress shoes: stiff, blocky black Naugahyde things with heels like cubes of steel. Generic navy-blue socks midway up the shin. But it was the wrong thing to tell Coach Applegate. If I had been quiet, I may have gotten away with languishing all game at the end of the bench. Instead, he started me at point guard. To rub it in he had me jump the ball to start the game.

EDDIE CHUCULATE

"Look at the shoes that kid's got on!" I heard someone yell as
soon as I clopped onto the shiny maple floor, which was followed by
shouts and laughter.

I of course lost the jump and spent the next couple of minutes
clomping along like a Clydesdale, sliding with no traction, balls
bouncing off my head, dribbling off my foot out of bounds. Every
time I touched the ball a whistle blared for something: double dribble, traveling, carrying. Laughter filled my cranium and echoed off
the rafters. School officials in ties and referees had smirks on their
faces, pointing and shaking their heads.

Applegate called time out and without even looking at me
subbed me out with Glen Lafitte, the starting point guard and my
secondary mate in football. We already trailed 10–0 thanks to that
stunt. That was my last game of organized basketball. I would have
left town if the game had been in Tish because Denise, as cheer-
leader, and Lisa would have been there. That night, though, I was
back in the backyard, draining free throws and sticking imaginary
buzzer-beating jumpers.

1978-79

CHAPTER 21

A WEEK AFTER we saw *Jaws*, Cousin Bud and Uncle Roston came from Calera in an unexpected visit to take me fishing. I was supposed to meet Lisa, so while they were sitting on the couch, I slipped out the back door, got on my bike, and raced over to her house. I told her I was going fishing and would come by later. When I got back home, everyone was wondering where I'd went. While Bud and Roston waited on the sofa in the living room, Momma pulled me into her bedroom out of their earshot.

"Eddie, you're going to have a lot of girlfriends in your life, but your cousin will always be your cousin," she said. "That was rude. Now get in there and say you're sorry."

She was right. A few days later I rode by Lisa's to find a vacant house. Neighbors outside watering their yard told me they moved to Texas.

We went fishing at a narrow creek that S-curved lazily and vanished behind a stand of blooming dogwood on the Blue River north of Tishomingo. The explosion of white-pink on the trees meant sand bass were running on Pennington Creek, but here we were after channel cats. From the bridge we saw the fish rise and fan their tail fins, drawing rings on the surface that spread in a widening bull's-eye. Pink blooms drifted onto the water, twirled, and floated with the current. Tilting bottom side up suddenly, a duck plunged its head under, dirty-white fanny flashing and orange web feet kicking for balance.

On the bank, the trick was to cast upstream at the right angle and distance for the current to drift the bait into the hole. We were using frozen whole shrimp out of the box we bought from Larry's IGA. A barrel-shaped slip sinker provided the weight—too heavy and your line sank where it hit the water, too light and it floated past the target and rested uselessly in the shallows.

Above, a pickup crossed the bridge—thunk THUNK, thunk THUNK—over a loose section of boards. My first cast was too far upstream, floating back only a few yards before sinking shy of the hole. I switched to a lighter lead and threw in again. The current pulled my line directly over the hole. The slack line drew taut, and my pole bent so severely I thought it would snap. Line zipped from my reel in a high-pitched whine and adrenaline shot through me like I'd stepped on a rattlesnake.

I felt the fish's vibrating tug through the pole as the line raced back upstream from the direction it came. I gave the rod a short jerk to assure the hook was set and the fish made a series of spastic moves to shake it: racing in counterclockwise and clockwise circles, speeding toward, then directly away from me, diving deep, then racing downstream with the current.

My line was tight and at a high angle out of the creek. Water dripped from it, catching the sun. The fish began to tire but his repeated charges for the depth of his hole—and probably a log he would tangle my line around—still popped my rod tip although he could no longer make the drag sing.

I began to reel him in four or five revolutions at a time, taking up slack, with the tip pointed at the water, then dragging him along by pulling the pole over my shoulder. I began to see flashes of his white belly. Still, though, he fought, jerking his head violently left and right like a dog with a toy, and flipping. With the rod in my left hand held away from my body I was able to drag him to my feet, reach down, and with three fingers in his mouth lift him flopping from the water.

He clamped down and I felt the ridges of his teeth—sharp but not painful—top and bottom. Such thrashing from larger specimens has sprained wrists and left blood. I laid him in grass away from the rocky bank for fear he would flip back in. He bucked once or twice, sides heaving, then lay motionless, lidless eyes like drops of motor oil.

His black whiskers curled from the sides of his flat head into the grass. He let out a croak. His top horizontal half was a glossy moss green; the bottom was light cream with a long deep-forked tail. I ran a nylon cord through his stark-white gills, and built a small pool lined with rock to contain him.

Bud must have seen the battle, for he jogged my way from downstream and under the bridge with his smaller catch. Roston came from upstream carrying a hoe and a brown grocery sack full of wild onions with their dirty white bulbs spilling over. He took his own pole from the bank and we spent the rest of the afternoon going up and down the creek, drifting the shrimp into the holes.

We each caught three or four more until the shrimp ran out. They wouldn't bite the crawdads we seined, the red wiggler worms we picked by flipping over rotting logs, or the grasshoppers we caught in the adjacent field, but they could not resist the shrimp. Bud landed a fat bluegill on a kicking yellow hopper and we strung it up, too. Roston said we had caught enough anyway, and we scrambled back up the hill to the truck with Roston carrying the stringer of about a dozen big catfish.

CHAPTER 22

WHEN MOMMA FOUND out that my dad had a decent-paying job for the city of Tulsa, she filed to get child support for me and Dawn. With that came visitation rights for Shorty, but more appropriately for Grandma Chuculate, who never let my dad forget he was entitled to them. Until then, my dad was only mentioned to me in occasional birthday notes from her. We began every-other-month trips to Tulsa—long, three-hour car rides. They were one-sided visits, too, because he never came down to see us on the opposite months. Probably had no idea where Tishomingo was.

Riding along the sweeping cloverleaf interchanges that rose curving into the sky like a ride at the fair with cars, pickups, and semis shooting off in all directions underneath and glittering downtown skyscrapers above, I was fascinated by the big city, and hooked. It was quite a sight for someone who just a few years ago walked across a dirt road to use the bathroom in an outhouse and saw a black snake at the bottom of the hole flicking a red tongue at him.

The names along the highway enthralled me: Crosstown Expressway, Skelly Drive, Beeline, Admiral, Lewis, Harvard, Yale, Tulsa Zoo, Tulsa International Airport, Gilcrease Museum, Keystone Dam, Bell's Amusement Park, Woodland Hills Mall; big

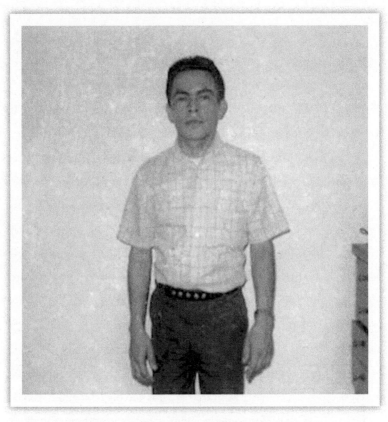

Shorty around 1968, age 24. In addition to cutting hair, he was also a talented guitarist who played by ear. A couple of his favorite songs were "Lay Down Sally" and "Bony Maronie." (Courtesy of the author.)

green signs that read like a puzzle such as I-244/I-444 with arrows pointing to other big cities like DALLAS/OKC, KANSAS CITY, and ST. LOUIS. Fire trucks with swirling sirens honked past us and I felt like I was in a dream. There would be so much to do here, I thought.

But when I finally arrived at Grandma Chuculate's in the projects on Commodity Hill, reality and the stuffy smell slapped me in the face. There was Grandma in her gown, slippers, and walking chair with yellow tennis balls on the front legs and little doilies everywhere: a dim, muted existence with Oral Roberts preaching on the radio. "Something *good* is going to happen to you today," he always said, reminding listeners that only what you give can multiply, then he gave out *his* address. I didn't want to hear all that: I wanted to be at the zoo, the mall, the lake, the downtown ice-skating rink, riding the Zingo roller coaster, or watching baseball at Drillers Stadium, the biggest ballpark I'd ever seen.

If we were lucky we got to do one of those things. Sometimes the big excursion of the trip would be riding the city bus with Shorty to OTASCO on Southwest Boulevard, where promises of a new mountain bike devolved into a rod and reel, which I didn't get to use until we returned to Tish.

I tried calling him "Dad," but it just didn't sound right after all these years of not having one, so I stuck with "Shorty." Sitting, he'd pull me to him, and I'd relent to the rough whiskers, the sour breath, the incomprehensible language: "I love you, son, don't you ever forget that, you hear? Tell your mother I'll always love her."

I spent a lot of time on these visitation-rights outings holed up in the apartment reading. At twelve, I read the paperback *Helter*

My dad and me in Muskogee around 1969. Shorty was a barber who worked alongside his father, the Rev. Edward Chuculate, in shops in the Cherokee Nation of northeast Oklahoma, including the towns of Jay and Stilwell. (Courtesy of the author.)

Skelter, which started off by saying "The story you are about to read will scare the hell out of you." I'd walk down the big hill on Union Avenue to the branch library with dad's fraternal twin, Uncle "Bigboy" Bill, and check out a pile of books.

There was only so much you could do there on the outskirts of the city. I couldn't just get on a bus on my own; no telling where I'd wind up. Shorty worked during the week for the street department and would be gone all day, too tired to do anything when he got back. One Saturday he took me riding, stopping by the liquor store, then on to some city tennis courts near downtown. We sat in the car for a while, then went home because he said there weren't any women playing. No swimming, skating at the Williams Center, or eating hot dogs at the Drillers game we never made it to.

One night the Tulsa phone book with Yellow Pages caught my eye. It looked a foot high compared to the little Tishomingo directory, where we were listed under *Lori Green* and were always getting calls for *Green Light Auto*, one above. No, we didn't have an alternator belt for a '73 Monte Carlo. The Tulsa book had reams of pages of names in fine print on thin paper that reminded me of a Bible. Then a big section in yellow with names of businesses.

I began reading it like a book, starting with the emergency numbers inside the front cover, with tips on avoiding shocking yourself or who to call if you accidentally drank poison. I scanned the map of the United States with all the area codes sectioned off. Oklahoma had two: 918 and 405, splitting the state east and west.

Bigboy came into the room and joked with me.

"What page you on in your book there, Eddie?"

After everyone went to sleep I came to the section on how to make international calls: Canada, Australia, the UK, Germany, France, Mexico. I saw names that sounded like Oklahoma under the Japan entry, so I called Yokohama.

It wasn't simply punching in seven digits. You had to enter 1, then another code, then another, then hit seven more random buttons. I got several recordings saying the "call cannot be completed as dialed" before I heard ringing. No answer. But this fueled my determination. I tried several more numbers before I got an answer.

"Moshi moshi," a female voice answered, clear as Ma Bell.

"Hello, I'm calling from Oklahoma," I said, thinking everyone in the world spoke English and if they didn't, they'd understand if I talked slow.

The receiver uttered a few more incomprehensible phrases and I stuck with "I'm calling from Oklahoma," enunciating as if talking to a three-year-old.

She hung up. Not letting this stop me, I received a few more answers and hang ups before entering a semiconversation.

"Moshi moshi," a male voice answered.

"Hi, I'm calling from Oklahoma."

"Yokohama?"

"O-kla-ho-ma," I said, emphasizing each syllable.

"Yokohama?"

"Oklahoma."

I heard chattering, then he handed the phone off.

"Moshi moshi," a female voice said.

"I'm calling from Oklahoma."

"Yokohama?"

"Oklahoma."

The phone was handed around to several people that time, and I heard several other Japanese phrases in questioning tones, but we never got past the "Yokohama-Oklahoma" exchange. Finally, they hung up.

Momma picked me up the next weekend to go back to Tishomingo. Driving down the highway, she asked if I had a good time.

"I guess. We rode the bus to OTASCO and we went and watched tennis one day."

"Tennis?"

"Downtown. But we left because there weren't any women playing."

"Hmmm."

We had reached Okmulgee and were waiting at a stoplight. She was silent, tapping her cigarette ash out the window.

"Oh, yeah," I said, remembering. "He said to tell you he'll always love you."

"Oh, bull," she said, and rolled her eyes. She turned up the radio and drove on at the green light.

It was sort of embarrassing to tell her that because we weren't a family that went around spouting the l-word left and right.

A few weeks later I called him.

"The number you have reached is no longer a working number. Please try your number again or call the operator for assistance. Goodbye."

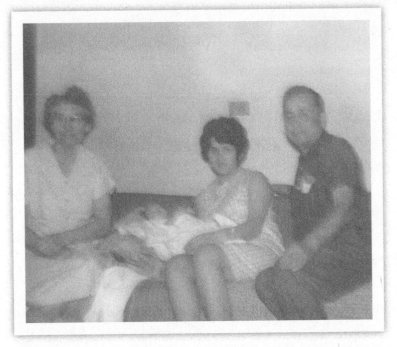

My grandmother Martha (Lundbeck) Chuculate of Litchville, North Dakota, and grandpa Ed Chuculate with me and Momma shortly after my birth. As a missionary in 1932, Martha was dispatched to Bamako, Mali, where she helped establish a church and Sunday school in the region. Upon her return in 1937, she was sent to Adair County, Oklahoma, where she met and married Ed, a Baptist preacher. (Courtesy of the author.)

Grandma's phone had been disconnected after she received a bill for hundreds of dollars. Her entire monthly pension—minus an Oral Roberts donation—didn't even cover it. Shorty didn't care; he'd lived most of his life without a phone anyway. And Momma sure wasn't going to pay it.

CHAPTER 23

OVER SEVENTH AND eighth grades in Tishomingo, I was settling in and others were becoming the new kids in town for a change. In social studies, I finished off every class period by repeating a joke I'd heard the night before on *The Tonight Show Starring Johnny Carson*, which came on at ten thirty after the news. Mr. Houser didn't seem to mind, since they usually concerned current events like an oil spill or hijinks at the White House. Michelle Byars told the teacher that her grandma said a tornado went right through downtown Tishomingo one year.

"Did it stop at all the stop signs?" I cracked.

In math, Mrs. Rowland would have two students stand at the chalkboard and write down the problem, like "what's 410 x 82," as she announced it, and whoever finished first won.

I approached the board and Mark Slover, our quarterback on the football team, said under his breath, "Get 'em, Chuculate, get 'em!" like siccing a dog on someone. I was lightning quick, finishing off the problem, "33,620," in a flurry of carry-over marks, underlining the answer with a flourish, snapping the chalk in the process, and spinning back to face Mrs. Rowland. It got my heart racing.

In football I had a little speed, could catch the ball, and displayed some natural athletic ability. Coach Upton put me in the secondary, where I did OK but had a problem with yanking face masks: They were just too irresistible and convenient. After I'd cost us several fifteen-yard penalties, he'd seen enough.

To close off practice he huddled us up on second-string offense and told us to run "22," a simple handoff calling for the 2 back, which was me at tailback, to run between the 2 hole, the gap between the center and right guard.

Then he went over to the first-string defense and told Todd May, a starting linebacker about six feet tall who already sported a mustache and legally rode a motorcycle to school, what the offensive play was and to stick to Chuculate as hard as he could. Supported by two teammates, I awoke to the sound of cleats clacking on asphalt on the way to the locker room. I still held the ball, however. Coach Upton had found his kickoff and punt returner.

The next game at home against Kingston was my first assignment in the role. Upton lectured us against catching any punt within our own 5-yard line, much less in the end zone, and to just back off from it. On my first chance my baseball instincts took over and I caught the ball a yard deep in the end zone, took off, and was gang-tackled at the 1. We had first and 99 yards to go.

On the sidelines Upton grabbed me by the face mask to get my attention, a little of my own medicine, I presume.

"What did I just tell you!" he growled, then let me go. That was the end of my kickoff-return career.

In PE, Upton paired the seventh graders against one another in boxing. He carried a boxful of gloves and headgear to the front lobby of the new gym, where he squared us off. I was pitted against my good friend Louis Lackey since we were about the same size and height.

We drew after three rounds, neither of us getting off any clean shots, spending most of the time staggering in circles in a bear hug. We were sweating and sucking air when it was over, embracing like we had just suffered through an epic fourteen-round Thrilla in Manila.

For my next bout Upton matched me against Darrell, an eighth grader. He looked older, too, like a car mechanic, but was shorter than me by a head so I thought I should be able to take him. I wound up to hit him and he peppered me twice on the nose, bringing water to my eyes and a roaring waterfall sound between my ears. Shouts from classmates and Upton sounded miles away in a tunnel. I shook my head like a dazed animal and the headgear slipped over my eyes.

I tried to adjust the padded helmet with my hands but there were no fingers to work with. Darrell cracked me in the ribs, and when I bent over in pain, he popped my jaw with an uppercut, snapping my head back and staggering me out of bounds. Upton caught me.

"You OK, son?" he said, putting my mouthpiece back in. I shouldn't have, but I nodded.

I swung at Darrell and he ducked. I swung again and he ducked. I wished I were waltzing around the floor with Louis again. Darrell went at me methodically, jabbing, punching, not breaking a sweat. I lasted the three rounds with him, miraculously, and we tapped gloves when it was over. That was the only time I touched him. It was like Upton had gone out and found a Golden Gloves boxer and slipped him into our group.

In class I walked up to Upton and told him I wouldn't be there the next day because my grandpa had died. It was true; I was going to Grandpa Green's funeral in Calera.

Sitting behind his desk, with his mustache giving him a frowning visage, Upton said, "I'm real sorry to hear that, son." He had an intense stare. I got the feeling that he knew Grandpa Green and was shocked to hear about it.

I was prepared for him to say "OK" dismissively, or just nod and not even look up, but the way he regarded me levelly with direct eye contact, I could tell he really meant it, and it made me feel sad that I should feel worse than I already did.

CHAPTER 24

RIDING AROUND WITH Gary after school we passed a nice brick home near a spread of shade trees. Gary stopped.

"That's where the Chicago Bears coach lives," he said.

"Oh, bull," I said.

"Yeah, my dad told me. His name's Neill Armstrong."

Everybody knew Neil Armstrong was the spaceman.

"Not the man on the moon," Gary said. "The football coach."

What would the Chicago Bears head coach be doing living in Tishomingo? I thought.

"Let's check him out," I said.

We laid down our bikes and walked up to the front door. To my surprise, there was a Chicago Bears decal stuck on the glass on the upper corner. I knocked. A tall, slender man in gray sweats answered.

"Are you the coach of the Chicago Bears?" I asked, point-blank.

"Well, yes, I am," he said. "Who let that secret out?"

"Gary here told me."

"Well, Gary here is right. Not the man on the moon."

He told us to come on in. He said he was from Tishomingo "like you" and led us over to a small office in the corner off the dining room.

"You boys play football?"

"Yes, sir," we answered in unison.

"What positions?"

"Safety," I said.

"Split end," Gary answered.

"So did I," the coach said. "Tishomingo High School."

He pawed around in his desk and signed two team photos and gave us folders embossed with the Bears logo containing schedules and a roster. A big picture of star running back Walter Payton was included in the publicity material.

It was a quick but mind-boggling visit. He was real nice, busy it seemed, but took time out for two local kids. I rode home and told Momma I'd just met Neill Armstrong. She was skeptical, too, until I showed her the photos and signature.

"He lives just a few blocks from school," I said.

I tried to become a Bears fan but I was just too hooked on Roger Staubach, Tony Dorsett, and the Dallas Cowboys. I had a picture of Staubach taped to the door of my room striking a passing pose with a stamped autograph. I knew it was stamped because it didn't smear when I wiped it with a licked fingertip. The Cowboys sent it after I wrote a fan letter that began, "Dear Roger Staubach, How are you? I am fine." The Bears never came on TV anyway unless they were playing Dallas.

My great-grandma Frances, superstitious and skeptical, always told us the moon landing was a hoax. A couple of guys in costumes bouncing around for cameras in a studio. She also thought newscasters on TV were following her around the room, since every time she moved from her chair to the bed, there they were staring right at her again. But I began to think she might be right. Neill Armstrong wasn't an astronaut, he was the coach of the Chicago Bears.

There weren't any jobs for Momma in Tish and Roman's work was spotty and usually out of town. He had a job in Norman on a Saturday and I rode with him, anxious to see the University of Oklahoma for the first time.

At the jobsite near campus was an athletic field surrounded by tall green shrubbery, which blocked the view inside. Towering stadium lights loomed overhead and I heard shrill whistles and yelling and clapping. The Sooners were practicing football! I finally had a chance to see them after years of watching on television or listening on the radio.

Roman let me walk the few blocks over to investigate. I came back sooner than expected.

"Well, what'd you see?" Roman asked.

"Aw, just a bunch of guys playing soccer," I said.

Roman didn't get paid for his job right off so he came up with an idea. Since there were so many neighboring yards in Chickasaw Nation housing, I went around knocking on doors to see if anybody wanted their lawn mowed. There were two rows of about ten houses each. They all looked the same except their brick color alternated light red or dark red. We had light red.

I dragged the mower up and down both roads, but either no one was home, they didn't need it, or told me to check back next week. The only taker was Roman's cousin Dorothy on the far end of the opposite row. She lived alone with her son Jonathan, who was a few grades under me in school.

Just my luck her grass was about knee high in back and looked about as big as the football field across the street. Roman helped me get started, then went home. It took forever. The mower kept chugging out and if I couldn't get it started on my own, I had to walk back and get Roman, who'd restart it.

Then it ran out of gas. We didn't have any at home so Dorothy drove to the station and filled a gallon can. Jonathan even mowed a few laps. It got so clogged underneath I'd have to turn it over on its side and claw out the grass around the wheels and blade, which was probably dull as a butter knife. Homer always kept his blade sharp, unbolting it and sharpening it with a file.

Everyone was waiting when I returned with the fifteen dollars around sunset. It took all day to get the one yard mowed. We went to Larry's IGA and Momma got hamburger meat and Hamburger Helper, some pop, a box of vanilla wafers, pickle loaf and white bread, and potato chips, and she put a couple of dollars in the tank. I think Roman was getting a check on Monday, so I saved us that time.

CHAPTER 25

THROUGH HER MARRIED friends Mel and Larry in town, Momma got a job in Sherman, Texas, at Texas Instruments, soldering semiconductor chips. She carpooled with them, leaving when it was still dark at five thirty in the morning for the 220-mile round trip. They took turns driving.

The job at TI paid well but it seemed to me a long way to travel for a job. Before her first check came, she called to me as I was shooting baskets in the backyard.

"Eddie, do you know those neighbors over there? Ever talk to them?"

I went over to the back window carrying my basketball. She was talking to me through the screen as she sat in a kitchen chair smoking a cigarette. She was referring to the adjacent house to the north, which wasn't part of the Chickasaw development and was surrounded by a chain-link fence, one of the original properties on the land. I didn't know them.

"You think you could go over there when it's dark and get some apples from their tree?"

At first it sounded simple but the way she was talking

conspiratorially in a hushed tone gave me pause. And why at night? I bounced the ball.

"Yeah, I guess so," I said, wondering why the sudden big deal about apples. "How many?"

"Oh, five or six oughta be enough."

I shot free throws and lay-ups until it grew dark, then kicked the ball over the fence. The light from their kitchen window created a small yellowish patch in the yard. I stuffed apples off the ground into my windbreaker pockets and in my pants but when we looked at them in the glare of the kitchen light, they were rotten and mushy. Their green skins had orange holes. Momma cut one open and found a small white worm.

I threw them across the road and went back for more. Their house was still quiet. I was going to say I was just getting my ball if someone came out. I probably could have just asked them for a few apples, but by now it felt like some sort of test, and I wanted to pass the test for Momma. I jumped and snatched a fat one, the limb springing back and thumping a few more onto the ground. These proved satisfactory. I jogged back feeling sort of heroic, like when I mowed the lawn for fifteen dollars.

Momma had a bag of flour and pie crusts that had been in the freezer since Christmas thawed out on the counter. She wasn't the master cook Granny was and made no secret of it. She asked me and Dawn what else could go into it.

"Sugar," Dawn said.

"Cinnamon," I offered, and got the bottle out of the pantry.

Momma washed and peeled the apples and cut them into slices.

I tried one. It was juicy and crunchy, but tart, making my eyes squint. She poured milk into the flour and let Dawn stir it up and dump in the sugar. I added the cinnamon powder. When it seemed about the right consistency we added the slices and mixed them in.

She baked it and that's all we had for dinner that night. It tasted nice and sweet and cinnamony and a little sour. Missy began eating it with her fingers and got it all over her face. Rather than neat triangular slices, it came off in globs, but I treated it as some sort of special occasion, which it was in retrospect. In the morning we rode with Momma to Sherman to collect her first check, going through Milburn, Durant, Calera and crossing the long Red River bridge.

There was the big WELCOME TO TEXAS sign on the right with the red, white, and blue flag and single white star. Soon, we were in Denison and after another highway bridge, suddenly in Sherman. She parked in a big lot outside TI and we waited while she went in for her check. After the bank, the first stop was a Tastee-Freez for hamburgers. After getting groceries in Tish, we unloaded them at the house. When I went out back to shoot baskets, I couldn't find my ball. I went inside and looked in my room, then remembered kicking it over to the neighbor's. I went into the yard and there sat the basketball on our side of the fence next to a sack of newly picked green apples.

After the money started rolling in, Momma surprised me with a new pair of jeans. We had already done our back-to-school shopping in Ada because there weren't any sizable department stores in Tishomingo. Indian kids had their school supplies like notebooks, crayons, markers, compasses, protractors, and pens and pencils covered through a program called Johnson-O'Malley (JOM), where you produced a voucher at the store, but clothes I guess were your own responsibility.

I'd usually get a couple pairs of pants and dress shirts and new shoes. I asked Momma for white Converse Pro Leather with the red star and chevron I saw Dr. J wear in ads in *Sports Illustrated*, but I wound up with something from Payless. By then there was also Dawn, Anthony, and Missy to worry about in the shoe department. I returned from Ada with a pair of new corduroy pants and dress shirts and shoes to start the school year, but after the first few days reverted to jeans, T-shirts, and old low-top basketball shoes, which Granny called "tennies."

Momma came back from work with the new jeans in a sack, tired of seeing me wearing my ripped and faded pairs. Happy, I ran into the bedroom and tried them on. Size twelve, they fit perfectly, but flared at the bottom so wide they covered my shoes. They looked absolutely ridiculous. I wouldn't be caught dead in them. I took them off and put my old ones back on.

"What's wrong, they too big?" Momma said.

"Little long at the bottom," I said, handing them back to her in the bag and trying to get out the door without further discussion.

"Maybe I can hem them up," she said. "Put them back on and let me see."

I put them on again, wincing at the belled bottoms some people called "elephant ears." They were normal until just after the knee until they widened out dramatically, brushing the floor.

"There's nothing wrong with those," Momma said. "Turn around. Let me see."

I spun on the slick living room tile, elephant ears flapping.

"They fit perfect," she said. "I might even get a pair. They're on sale at TG&Y in Denison."

"Momma, they're like *Soul Train*. Nobody wears these." I flopped down on the sofa.

Hearing *Soul Train*, she started dancing around in the kitchen, putting up groceries.

"Oh, bull," she said. "Everybody wears them. It's just a pair of jeans. Wear them tomorrow."

She was already gone in the morning when I left for school, but I dutifully wore them, felt her watching me while I dressed even though she was probably in Texas by then. I didn't make it two blocks before the elephant ear on the right got caught in my chain, tearing a small hole and leaving a grease stain, and I nearly wrecked.

I arrived at school feeling like I was under a spotlight. I kept looking at people to see if they were staring at my jeans, but no one was paying attention. No one said a thing, but I was relieved when I finally took them off for football practice.

I wore gym shorts home, stuffing the bell-bottoms in my bag. Momma never said anything after that or asked and I never wore them again. They languished in my drawer until I got scissors and made shorts out of them.

CHAPTER 26

NO ONE HAD a fence around their houses in the Chickasaw Nation projects, so we essentially had one giant backyard stretching a half mile, albeit with the occasional clothesline, basketball goal, or doghouse obstructions. I was the all-time quarterback, drawing up simple pitch plays in the huddle for Anthony. Anthony was three foot nine and forty-five pounds, and most players were afraid to tackle him before discovering they couldn't due to his speed.

I'd smack the ball with a "hut!" to start the play, pitch it to Anthony, make the first block, and watch him fly. Problem was, he didn't know when to stop and kept running: He ran through Charlie Carter's yard, through the Maytubbys', Imoticheys', and Bakens', clear to the end of the houses where the land reverted back to pasture. He ran long after players had quit chasing him. "Anthony the Bumble Bee," I christened him.

One of the regulars was Larry Reynolds. Larry was big for his seventh-grade frame, which made him slow for our brand of free-for-all, speed-counts style of playground football, but he lumbered after us just the same. Due to his size and an unfortunate body odor, sometimes the games devolved into personal attacks.

"Larry stinks!" we'd shout, and forget about the game, laughing and giggling while Larry chased us around the backyards. Even the little kids got into the fray, yelling "Larry smells like a dog!" or "Take a bath, Larry!" I knew I shouldn't be doing it, but I joined in the taunts. Larry was nice to everyone and just wanted to be part of the gang, part of the games, but the attacks were merciless and left him in tears, and he'd give up and stalk back to his house, wiping his nose on his shirtsleeve. At school, everyone got along fine.

We'd resume playing like nothing ever happened. Sure enough, Larry would be back out there the next day. At first we'd play like normal, then the taunts would begin again after Larry made a tackle. It was a wolf pack mentality: No one said anything until the first insult was launched, then everyone joined in and he'd start chasing us.

I was too limber and fleet for him to catch me. I whizzed by him, saying, "You stink!" and he stuck out a foot and tripped me. He pounced on me with his forearms crisscrossed against my neck, driving my face in the dirt.

"Say you're sorry!" he panted through gritted teeth, bangs of sweaty hair obscuring his eyes.

I couldn't really say anything at the moment.

"Say it!" he said, shoving harder.

I slapped at the ground.

"I'm sorry, Larry," I wheezed, and I truly was. I should have known better. I was older than everyone else and they copycatted my actions.

He let go while everyone watched, and as he got off me in stages, he drove his knee into my back in one last retaliation, knocking the breath out of me and banging my forehead into the ground and my teeth against my lip. Everyone scattered and I walked back home, dusting twigs and grass out of my face and hair. I spit red on the ground. That was the last time I ever said, "Larry, you stink!"

Riding my bike through an alley, I spotted a half-court smooth cement basketball court with painted lines, regulation glass backboard, and new stark-white nylon net. Even though I had quit the team, I still loved to play. Hidden from the streets by trees, it was part of construction of a new house that had been abandoned. No cracks on the court or bent, rusted rims without a net, no KEEP OUT signs or fences to crawl under. It was like a waterfall in the middle of a desert.

I told my former teammate Eddie Smith about it, and we started meeting there after school to play daily. No one else knew about the court. We kept it between us, so it was always just me and him. Tall and lanky and a wide receiver in football, he could dribble and shoot with either hand. We'd play to twenty-one by ones and have to win by two and I could never beat him. He'd dribble with his back to me down low, spin one way, and lay it in with the opposite hand. Or he'd dribble from the top of the key, fake like he was going to drive, and pull up and sink a seventeen-footer right in my face.

I'd try my best to beat him but often after he hit twenty-one, I'd get on my bike and ride off angry without even saying bye. But I'd come back the next day for more one-on-one and another beating. He was still on the team, getting better every day. What made it so frustrating is he made it seem effortless. I had to drive, dribble, grab my own misses, shoot again, miss, shoot again, and he'd swat it out of bounds.

*   *   *

Gary lived just down the street from the hidden court, and I'd go to his house and listen to 1950s music. When I lived in Muskogee, every Sunday night I tuned in to a golden oldies radio show on KBIX from nine to ten as I lay in bed. I heard "Splish Splash (I Was Takin' a Bath)," which began with gurgling water sounds, "Rock Around the Clock (Till Broad Daylight)," or "All I Have to Do Is Dream (Dream, Dream, Dream)," which always put me to sleep. I looked forward to this ritual all week. But in Tishomingo when I turned the knob to the station, I found a Texas Rangers baseball game or gospel music.

Gary had a vast collection of fifties albums handed down from his mom. We spent hours listening to "Yakety Yak (Don't Talk Back)," "Charlie Brown (He's a Clown)," Elvis, Buddy Holly, and Fats Domino. It's a wonder we didn't start greasing our hair in duck-tails and wearing Levi's with rolled-up cuffs. We'd go straight from the middle school and down the hill after class and listen until his mom came home from work at five. She was always in a good mood and happy to see me and I'd stay and eat dinner with them before biking home in the twilight. The first thing she did after she put up her coat and laid her bags down was start making dinner.

"I already ate at Gary's," I'd tell Momma.

Gary was also an avid reader and we competed to get the highest scores in English, raking in 90s and 100s on papers and getting mostly A's with an occasional B on our report cards. We never missed school and were always on the honor roll. That's why it was such a shock to everyone when we snuck in and destroyed the band room at the high school.

CHAPTER 27

I WAS STILL keeping the hidden court a secret, so Gary and I walked down the road and up the hill to play Horse one evening at our middle school. The goals were on an asphalt slab on school grounds, enclosed on all sides by buildings and obstructed from street view. I was trying to finish him off with the "e" with my backward free-throw shot but it glanced off the rim, hit a rock, and rolled toward the main building. Gary chased it down.

"Hey, this window's open," he said, picking up the ball.

I trotted over and saw that it was raised by about a foot. All the others were closed. We stared at it for a few seconds.

"Everyone's long gone," he whispered, reading my mind.

Instead of closing it and notifying someone or ignoring it and just finishing our game, we raised the window and crawled in. We ran up and down the halls for no particular reason, peeking into vacant classrooms, then went into the home-ec room and threw flour we found in a cabinet all over the kitchen, emptying the bag on countertops, the stove, and floor, and crawled back out.

I didn't wake up that morning thinking I was going to sneak into the school, much less vandalize it, but it was exciting to see what it looked like with no one in it. Eerie, yet fun. I felt it gave me some sort of advantage—access and knowledge no one else had. It was so easy I regretted not staying longer to snoop around.

A few days later I was leaving the Murray State student union after playing pinball when I heard yelling and clapping from afar. I rode around campus to investigate, following my ear, and saw a baseball game in progress in the distance. It was a stunner: It had never occurred to me that the school had a team. There was no Little League in Tishomingo—that's why I returned to Muskogee in the summer—and no middle school team, so the town was a baseball void in my life until I saw the junior college squad. I rode over and watched a few innings.

I went back the next day after school, but the field was totally vacant. It was on the outskirts of campus on the edge of town next to a seldom-used gravel road, seemingly carved out of pasture. Dorms, the student union, and gym were blocks away. I was about to leave when I saw a baseball behind the backstop.

Of course, I ran over to get it—baseball hound that I was—and on the way back saw a blue door on the side of the concession stand. I wondered if it would be unlocked like the window at the middle school. I knew I shouldn't, but I twisted the knob and it opened. In the semidarkness I saw rakes, a wheelbarrow, coiled-up water hoses, and bags of sand. As my eyes adjusted, I also saw a pair of spikes and a baseball glove at about the same time I heard a car crunching gravel up the road where the pavement ended. I slammed the door, got on my bike, and rode home, passing the driver, who waved at me. I waved back with my ball.

I couldn't sleep that night thinking about the glove and baseball shoes. I already had a glove and baseball shoes, but this was a *college* glove and *spikes*, which I had been dreaming of for years, anxious to stop playing in plastic cleats.

Gary asked if I was coming over to listen to records after school and I told him no, that I had to mow the yard. Then I rode over to the field and stole the glove and shoes. No one was around so I parked my bike, walked in, and stuffed them in my backpack, racing home with my heart beating 100 miles an hour. I went into my bedroom and shut the door.

No one at home would think anything of my having baseball shoes and a glove. I sat on my bed and took them out and knew they were something special: a solid-leather Wilson A2000 glove, and a pair of leather Brooks spikes in Murray State Aggies blue, out of my league but almost my size. I pictured myself showing them to Lonnie back in Muskogee.

It was the first time I'd stolen anything. I had never even taken a piece of bubble gum from a store. It just never occurred to me. I reasoned that they must not have been that important to someone if they were just lying around in a darkened concession stand. I'd put them to good use right away that summer. I knew no one could afford to buy them for me and mentally added up how many fifteen-dollar knee-high lawns they amounted to. I quit counting after ten: way too many.

At home, Roman was helping coach soccer on teams Dawn and Anthony played on at fields at Murray State—I had no interest—

and Missy was still a year away from kindergarten. Momma was still working at TI and when she wasn't watering the sun-facing side of the brick house because she felt it kept it cooler, she taught Missy to say "supercalifragilisticexpialidocious." We laughed when Missy always got tongue-tied halfway through and Momma got her to start all over again.

Momma gathered us around the kitchen table for games of Boggle where we shook the lettered dice to see how many words we could find. Sometimes she confused our names. She'd yell for one of us but it sounded like one rapid-fire name like "Ant!Miss!Dawn!Edd!" and we'd all come to the kitchen to see what she wanted.

Meanwhile, in the free time I had without basketball practice and games, I continued sneaking into places. The new high school behind the house had just opened. I wasn't due to begin ninth grade there until next year, but I used to have a locker in the gym. I knew that one of the rear doors to the locker room didn't lock if you didn't pull it tight.

This gnawed at me at home. Since the middle school and concession stand were so easy to get into, the high school probably was too. Shooting baskets in the backyard after dinner, I could see the red door across the road. When it grew dark, I walked back over and tried the door, which appeared from the sidewalk to be airtight. It opened right up. I slipped in and shut the door. Without the chirping of shoes on the court, coaches yelling and blowing whistles, or players joking around in the locker room, it was so quiet I heard the second hand click on the wall clock.

I turned on a light in Applegate's office and went through his desk. I took a pack of watermelon Bubblicious gum and popped a couple in my mouth. There was an official copy of the state high school basketball rules and a referees' manual in a drawer, and I took those. There was a new leather game ball on his desk with the cursive black *Wilson* outlined in gold and I couldn't resist that, either. I went home and hid the ball in the carport storage, and in my room, I studied the manuals like I was preparing for a test.

I couldn't keep totally quiet about what I did, so I told Gary. He came over after school and I showed him the ball and manuals. We shot baskets in the backyard with my old rubber ball, leaving the Wilson in the storage room because the first thing Momma or Roman would ask would be, "Where'd you get the new ball?" I'd have to make something up, like the coach gave it to me, but that wouldn't work because they knew the story with the coach and that I wasn't on the team anymore, so I kept it hidden.

I'd been playing with the rubber ball so long it was totally slick. I didn't have a needle to pump it up, so in order for me and Gary to shoot I warmed it in the oven until it swelled. It whanged in the air almost over your head every time you dribbled. That was usually good for fifteen minutes until it went flat again, and I'd put it back in the oven.

I pointed out the red door to Gary. He followed my finger across the open field between two neighboring houses to the east.

"I stuck gum in the door jamb so it wouldn't lock."

"It sure looks locked," he said.

"It's not."

We started shooting again.

"What are we going to do in there?"

"Just look around," I said, sort of hoping he'd refuse and try to talk me out of it, but I knew I'd go anyway even if he didn't.

"Just look around? You already know what it looks like." He quit bouncing the ball, then looked up. "OK, but we won't take anything."

We shot until the sun went down and walked over. Making sure no cars were coming, I tugged the door handle, and we went in. It was dark and we bumped into each other trying to find a light, hushing each other. We found a switch and flinched in shock at two people staring at us. They were our own images in the big mirror in the weight room.

We started laughing, then hushed each other again, punching each other on the arm. There were the offices, the workout machines and barbells, and a big whiteboard where they drew plays and other information like reminders to get physicals and when the bus was leaving for games. Some joker would also draw the occasional obscene graffiti.

Beyond another door were the boys' lockers. Through this tunnel-like room the basketball court gleamed honey-gold under soft gym lighting. We observed the strips of masking tape above lockers that had my former teammates' names written on them: Gunter, Lafitte, Boone, Slover, Smith—the starting five. My name, which should have been between Claborn and Rushing—was stripped off above an empty locker.

We crossed the court, keeping in the shadows. There was a faint lemon fragrance like it'd just been waxed. Gary looked at his watch and said he needed to be getting home, said his mom would be worrying. But instead of backtracking the way we came, we walked down a hall and through a set of doors and found ourselves in a room filled with musical instruments.

The Pride of Little Dixie performed at the Cotton Bowl football game every year in Dallas and was always winning awards. I heard the band practicing on the football field all the time. If not on the field, they marched on the grounds we'd just crossed surrounding the school. I probably knew their cadence as well as they did, hearing the drumbeats ricochet off our brick house nearly year-round.

Despite all that, I never knew this room existed. My classes were in the middle school and after basketball at the high school, I just got dressed in the locker room and went home. But here we were in the middle of it all. We couldn't resist and banged on a drum or two, crashed a couple of cymbals, the sounds deafening in the silence. This seemed to ignite us. I kicked a big bass drum and it responded with a thunderous boom. I kicked it harder, and my foot went through the skin.

Gary blew through a horn but couldn't get a sound, cheeks puffed like a chipmunk and face turning red. Inspired by my damage to the drum, he smashed the horn against a xylophone. I picked up a guitar and slung it against the wall. He slammed a tuba on the floor. We went through the whole room battering instruments, throwing sheet music in the air, tipping over chairs and upending tables. Before leaving we stomped on a few of the tall hats they wore. I spit out the gum I was chewing, and it landed on a copper cymbal. In the locker room, as a coup de grâce, I wrote on the big whiteboard: *Looking for who's to blame? Blame coach Applegate, he left the door open.*

CHAPTER 28

OVER THE NEXT few days, I acted like nothing had happened. On Tuesday I went with Momma to Larry's IGA. While she shopped I played a few games of Space Invaders, then went to the magazine section in the rear. The blaring headline on the *Johnston County Capital-Democrat* on a wire rack stopped me in my tracks: "VANDALS DESTROY HIGH SCHOOL BAND ROOM." I picked it up. There was a big article and pictures of twisted instruments on the floor, the hole in the drum and a close-up of the wad of gum on the cymbal. I put the newspaper back like it was on fire, glancing around to see if people were looking. I had already begun to think the whole thing was over when it was just beginning.

Since it had happened over the weekend, news was slow to trickle to the middle school. But after the paper came out that afternoon, it was all everyone was talking about. Rumors churned that it was Jack Hornbuckle because he had long hair and smoked cigarettes. Or it was Rowdy Robertson because he had been kicked out of band last year. Gary caught my eye in the hall. He just shook his head with a grim expression: no more giggling around and punching each other. In class, Mr. Miller had everyone take out a piece of paper. "Write down anything you know about what happened in the band room at the high school," he said.

I felt pressure as a top English and writing student to absolve Gary and me with an ironclad statement. I wrote that we were shooting baskets in my backyard after dinner. We heard what sounded like drums booming and crashing from the high school. Assuming the band was practicing, we thought nothing of it. I lived next to the school, and they were always practicing, I wrote. We did see, I continued, Rowdy Robertson and his friends riding around the school on their bikes. It was getting dark, and I had homework to do, so Gary went home and I went inside. Other than that, all I know is what I read in the paper, I said.

I should have written that I didn't know anything, which is probably what everybody else wrote, because they *didn't* know anything. And I shouldn't have said anything about Gary. Before class was over, I was pulled out and led to the principal's office by Mr. Miller. From there it was determined I should talk to the police. The last time I set foot on Tishomingo school property was stepping off the curb into a squad car to go downtown.

They had me sit on an iron cot in a cell near the chief's office. I wasn't handcuffed or anything and they left the door open, so I assumed it was just scare tactics. I wasn't scared yet, still thinking it was all going to blow over. I just had to stick to my story. I heard someone talking on the phone and a few minutes later heard Roman's voice. He came down the hall and stood in the doorway.

"I never thought I'd see you in here," he said, chuckling. "Did you tear up the school the other day?"

"No," I said from the cot. He cocked his head at me briefly with a serious expression, then his smile returned. He probably saw right through me.

"Doesn't sound like you, but they sure think you did something," he said, tugging at a cell bar as if inspecting it for strength. He sighed. "Well, come on, they can't talk to you without me or your mother there and she's in Sherman. Just get in there and lie your butt off."

We bypassed the chief's office and some other doors for a windowless room with a small desk and folding chairs. The deputy who had driven me from school sat in the corner with his legs crossed, picking at his fingernails with a pocketknife. We sat across from the chief, who wore his name on a rectangular metal strip above his shirt pocket: Turner. He didn't say anything for a while, reading the paper I wrote in Mr. Miller's class. He laid the sheet down, took off his glasses, and leaned back. His leather gun belt creaked. The holster was empty, but a gold star was clipped on the side.

"So, tell me what happened, Mr. Chuculate."

I was ready.

"Nothing. Me and Gary were outside shooting baskets and heard some noise at the high school," I said, trying to remember exactly what I'd written. "We saw Jack Hornbuckle and some others riding around. It got dark and Gary went home, and I went inside. It's all right there."

He took the paper off the desk and looked it over again.

"Thought it was Rowdy," he said.

"Yeah, I meant Rowdy," I said quickly. "They were riding their bikes around the sidewalks at the gym."

He unwound the string on a manila envelope and took out a stack of photographs and pushed them over.

"Take a look at those and tell me if anything rings a bell."

They were individual black-and-white pictures of the hole in the drum, the cymbal on the floor with my gum on it, a guitar with its neck cracked and strings all haywire, a pancaked band helmet, a flute bent into a V-shape. Sharp and clear and filling their entire frames, the objects became real to me then.

The last one was a panorama showing all the destruction at once. With music stands, stools, speakers, and desks flipped, leaning against one another haphazardly, and papers and instruments flung about, it looked like the room had exploded. But unlike the other photos, I'd never seen this one before. The enormity of what I'd done sank in, and I knew I wasn't getting out of it. My hands trembled as I passed them on to Roman.

"I saw all that in the paper," I said, almost like a question.

The officers looked at each other, probably anticipating my answer.

"What about this?" He spun another across the desk right up to me. It showed the message I'd written on the locker-room board.

"Now, look at this." He handed me the paper I wrote that morning. "Tell me, did you ever go to Ravia schools? That's how they teach them to print their *a*'s."

Looking back and forth from my statement to Mr. Miller and the picture of the message on the board, I saw all the *a*'s I had written with the curling hoods on top. In addition to that, the handwriting was plainly identical.

"Never went to Ravia," I said, and took a deep breath. It felt good to tell the truth about something.

"So you're telling me you didn't do this?"

"No, I didn't, Chief Turner."

He stood and bent over the desk, staring me right in the eye. "That's not what Gary's telling us. We've got him right there in the other room. Don't we, Charlie?" The deputy nodded, tight-lipped, still picking at his fingernails.

I looked at Roman. He raised his eyebrows at me.

"Eddie," the chief said, "are we still going to blame Coach Applegate?"

I felt tears welling up but blinked them back, not wanting to cry in front of the three men. I admitted to it, and even told them about crawling into the middle school a few nights before. The deputy asked me if I took anything, and I said just rule books and a basketball. But that seemed important, and he had Roman go home and bring those back to the station. I told Roman where to find the basketball in the storage room. I sat there talking to them and writing out a confession with the manuals and the new Wilson staring back at me on the desk. While I'd read the manuals cover to cover, I never even shot one basket with the ball.

If I were younger, I probably would have been spanked with a belt. But Momma just lectured me about how she couldn't afford to even rent Dawn a flute to join the band, and there I go destroying thousands of dollars of instruments, racking up a bill she could never pay—a lot of fifteen-dollar lawns for me.

She took off work to drive me to court, shaking her head occasionally and muttering like she still couldn't believe it.

"Stupid, stupid, stupid," she said. Not that I was stupid, but what I had done was stupid. "You've got sense but not horse sense." A saying she must have picked up from Granny.

She stood with me before the judge. Gary and his mom were there at the next table. Our harshest punishment was being expelled from Tishomingo schools. We never went to juvenile detention: maybe because we had good grades and attendance and had never done anything like it before.

"One last thing," the judge said, then pointed his index fingers in opposite directions. "Split 'em up."

The last time I saw Gary we were in his front yard talking about the interrogation. I told him I had stuck to my story until they told me he was in the other room and had already confessed. Gary looked at me startled and said he wasn't at the jail until the day after me. They'd lied to me like I'd lied to them!

I was still trying to make sense of that when we saw someone walking down the road, coming from the middle school. It was around three, so school had just been let out. As the figure came closer, we realized it was Jack Hornbuckle, blue bandana looped around his head, long blond hair snaking over the shoulders of a black leather jacket. A silver chain dangled in a loop from his jeans. He pointed at us with his cigarette, nodding his head and smiling, but didn't stop walking.

"I'll get it next time, boys," he said affirmatively, blowing smoke in the air, and continued strolling down the middle of the street, buckled boots clomping on the asphalt.

If I didn't live right across the street from the school, would I have ridden my bike across town just to get into the gym? I don't think so. Certainly not with any plan to destroy the band room. Could it be that I was mad at the coach for the stunt he pulled at Madill, embarrassing me in front of the whole universe? Maybe. But that doesn't explain tearing up band instruments. Plus, I didn't really want to be on the team anyway. *His* team, at least.

At home in the evening lying on the bed I shared with Anthony, I tossed my slick ball in the air. If I hadn't quit the team, I thought, I'd have been practicing or at a game and not sneaking into places and stealing things. Despite the incident with the coach, I had just started feeling like I belonged, and my Tishomingo classmates would be forever. Now I was expelled.

At first, I thought it meant missing a few weeks of school, but Momma explained that I was kicked out forever. I thought about all the kids I'd never see again and the coaches and teachers I liked, like Upton. Momma said it beat going to jail. I pictured myself sitting on the iron cot for years with a bunch of kids in striped jumpsuits, scheming about what they were going to do to the school once they got out. Everyone comparing notes on how best to slip into schools and gyms, what to take and what to tear up. Knowing it's wrong but doing it repeatedly. Would I still have been in eighth grade when I got out? How many kids saw their lives frozen, destroyed, because of one terrible decision? I felt undeservedly lucky.

Outside, the drumbeats began again, echoing loudly off the house and through the open windows. In my mind I saw the musicians leave the field in formation, stepping and turning sharply to the cadence with their horns at attention. Across the gravel lot they marched, until the drummers stopped, and everyone emptied into the band room, a room I wished I had never entered, never violated, where the pristine instruments gleamed, and the drumbeat never stopped.

CHAPTER 29

GARY MOVED TO Madill while I transferred to nearby Milburn, a small county school about ten miles east down the highway. I rode every morning with a teacher who also lived in Tishomingo. I walked down the gravel road to the corner, and she picked me up next to the highway in a brown two-door Honda Civic. Heather Lofton rode with her, too. Heather was already about six foot tall, it seemed. Her dad was the women's basketball coach at Murray State and wanted her to play at Milburn, a perennial state championship contender.

One silver lining was I got to play baseball again, right off at the beginning of the school year as a ninth grader since Milburn competed in the fall and spring seasons. I came ready to play, too, sporting the Brooks spikes, which matched the Milburn blue, and the A2000 glove. I still had never told anyone about taking those. I took my first dip of Copenhagen from a senior who offered it to me right before I took my cuts in batting practice. After the third or fourth pitch, the tobacco went to my head and made me dizzy and I had to back out and spit it out.

I'm sure administrators knew the reason I had transferred from Tishomingo but most teachers and students didn't know and I was never singled out because of it. Future Farmers of America (FFA), Skoal, and country music were big things at Milburn and I learned to weld and judge pigs and write things like, "Granted, the Duroc is leaner in the hindquarters, but the Yorkshire is thicker in the shoulders and rump and will likely produce better cuts of roast and loin." In welding, I'd flip the mask over my eyes by nodding my head and join two small plates of metal by guiding the rod carefully down the middle, creating a seam, with sparks bouncing off my coveralls. I'd shine the bead on an electric grinder and present it to Mr. Ferris for inspection.

Kids there just didn't raise an animal at home for a project; many lived on surrounding farms or ranches with cows, sheep, horses, chickens, and pigs. They spent all year getting a heifer or hog ready for stock shows, guiding them around the ring with a long rod, rubbing their bellies with it. They clipped and groomed the cows' hair and sprayed and bobbed their tails. I was envious when I learned they sold the animals at those shows for thousands of dollars. My only animal at home in Tish was a house cat. I scraped up change and cut coupons out of magazines to buy it food.

Dawn, who was still going to school in Tishomingo, agreed to help me study for a test that required me to match cuts of meat from diagrams of swine and beef.

"Where does Canadian bacon come from?" I asked her.

"Canadian pig, I guess," she said.

Toward the end of the school year Roman disappeared again so the five of us were stuck at home without a vehicle. Momma borrowed her friend Mel's car and took me with her to look for him. After asking her in-laws in Calera, she learned he was in nearby Durant, capital of Bryan County and self-billed as the Peanut Capital of the World. After some searching, we saw our Pontiac parked in the lot of an apartment complex next to a car that Momma must have recognized.

I looked on bewildered as Momma blared her horn and—failing to get Roman to show himself—popped the hood on the unknown vehicle and in a rage ripped out all the spark plugs and any other visible wiring. Huffing and puffing, she asked me could I drive our car back to Tishomingo, following her in Mel's car. What was I going to do? Say no? I was willing to do it if only to get us out of this bizarre situation, but as a bonus we'd have our car back.

"I'll go slow, just follow me," she said. "You can do it."

I started it up with Momma's spare key. I had taken driver's ed at Milburn and driven a little around the country roads, down shady river valleys, and over bridges in a new car, so that helped. But steering the long, old Pontiac with wild play in the wheel down busy US 69 and onto the curvy state highway for thirty miles was different.

But Momma went slow, and I had no trouble following, hunched over and hugging the wheel with both hands like a farmer on a tractor, eyeing her red taillights. It was my first time driving at night and as I wondered whose apartment that was and why Roman hadn't come out, a driver flashed me with bright lights when I forgot to jab the dimmer switch on the floorboard.

If Momma was a wound-up rubber band, Roman was a loose ball of yarn. When there was some crisis going on in the house, he was content to kick back on the couch and watch a Western or laugh at Richard Pryor jokes. He spanked me just once in Muskogee when I was eight, but it was half-hearted, and I could tell he regretted it.

Momma sped up some as there was little other traffic, and before long we were at the junction in Milburn for the turn west and ten-minute drive back to Tish. I turned off the highway onto our gravel road and into the driveway and carport, ending my real-world driver's education class.

I now felt directly involved in Momma and Roman's conflict, whatever it was. As usual, I didn't know what was going on between them. It seemed their disputes were always offstage. I had never witnessed anything physical—maybe verbal spats now and then—but Roman never stormed around in an angry mood. If Momma would have told me, I probably wouldn't have understood anyway. It wasn't until I was older that she began confiding in me, and even then she wouldn't tell me things she told Granny. I just figured they'd get back together since they always did sooner or later.

CHAPTER 30

MOMMA WAITED A few weeks until we were out of school, and we moved back to Muskogee. There were never any moving companies or U-Haul vans associated with these moves. Just packing things into boxes and filling the trunk and interior with whatever fit. Trash bags bulging with clothes crammed up against the rear windows. Missy and Anthony went to stay with their grandma in Calera, so we were split up again. I didn't see Roman until years later after Momma had remarried. That fall, Muskogee High became my fourteenth school in nine years.

As was often the case, Dawn stayed with Momma while I lived with Granny and Homer. They had moved into town at 1500 East Broadway, a small duplex on the corner across from a Seventh-day Adventist church. Every Saturday you'd see the churchgoers across the street gathering for services, which was odd because I thought everyone went to church on Sunday.

Our neighbor was an elderly, small spry woman who wore black-heeled shoes that looked like little boots below the hem of her simple dresses. Her hair was always in a net. I found out she had a phone and would ask to use it. I even gave her number out to friends who'd call me before picking me up to go to a game or baseball practice. You'd hear her clomping along the porch before she knocked on our door to tell me I had a phone call, but she never seemed to mind.

I walked a few blocks to Alice Robertson Junior High to catch the bus to MHS. I took a bath in the mornings because we didn't have a shower. Dumping bowls of water over my head after shampooing, I sometimes left the house in a hurry and my hair froze in brittle strands before I got to the bus stop. Looking at my transcripts from Milburn, my counselor, Mrs. Avalon Reece, enrolled me in FFA again. But in a big school like Muskogee, maybe 10 percent of kids joined FFA, where in Milburn it was 99 percent.

I was eating at noon period when I heard a familiar shout above the lunchroom din.

"Chook!"

I looked up to see Lonnie pointing at me a few tables away, grinning. He grabbed his tray and came over and sat across from me. It had been a couple of years since I'd seen him. He had faint traces of a mustache and chin stubble. But it was the same old Lonnie, maybe a little taller and heavier. We performed our ritualistic handshake.

"You back for good this time?" he said, munching on a pizza slice.

"I hope so." He always knew that if he hadn't seen me in a while I was probably in Tishomingo.

A group of girls walked by.

"Hey, Sam," one of them said in a teasing voice, calling him by his nickname.

"Who's that?" I asked.

My senior picture at Muskogee High School in 1984. By then I was covering sports for the Muskogee Daily Phoenix. I believe I'm in a studio, but the background bears a resemblance to Honor Heights Park in Muskogee, home of the annual Azalea Festival in April.
(Courtesy of the author.)

"Aw, this girl I been talking to. Hey, where you staying? I know Granny and Homer done moved out that house. Ain't no one there."

I said I was living with them in town.

"O and Broadway on the corner, not too far from A.R."

"That's cool. Tell 'em I said hi."

"You playing baseball?"

"Naw, man, I ain't played since the last time we played. I go to vo-tech after this. Only come here in the morning," Lonnie said. He pushed his tray away, leaned back, and smiled at me. "I'm getting Daddy's old truck when I get my license next year. We'll go fishing for sure."

"Where?" I said, already anticipating it.

Lonnie, age eighteen, receiving his Muskogee High School diploma from board of education member Dr. Virgil Matthews in May 1985. There was never a question of Lonnie earning his degree as his mother, Dianne Hill, was a lifelong historian and educator who taught African American and Native American history, among other subjects, for Muskogee Public Schools. (Courtesy of Melita Griffith.)

"Anywhere. Lock and Dam 17, Jackson Bay, Spaniard Creek, crappie at Greenleaf. I know a bunch more ponds now. Anywhere."

The bell rang and we put our trays on the dishwashing table. Lonnie jogged off to catch his ride to the vo-tech. It felt good to see him again, and as the semester wore on I began seeing more and more people I remembered from elementary and junior high. It was definitely better than being the brand-new kid again.

I'd walk down the hill from the gym and watch the Roughers practice baseball. They already had two or three guys at every infield position, slick-fielding shortstops turning double plays and making long, accurate throws to first. Meanwhile, a squad of outfielders caught fly balls fired rapidly out of a pitching machine while several pitchers threw along the side to several catchers, balls popping mitts in succession with coaches observing nearby.

It looked like a professional organization, not like in the summer when our coach stood at home plate in work boots hitting grounders and flies to everyone while chomping on a cigar. You'd go five or ten minutes before you had a ball hit to you, chewing on grass and looking at clouds. Muskogee was in the top size classification in Oklahoma while Milburn was in the smallest, and I didn't think I was good enough for a big-school team.

I only played Knothole ball the next two summers until my friend Spencer Wilkinson, a Creek and Arikara who was the main starting pitcher for MHS and a pro prospect, convinced me to go out for the high school team my senior year. But waiting so long hurt my chances as most of the team had already been together over their sophomore and junior seasons, and there was only one varsity spot available with three players including me competing for it.

The twenty-fifth and final position was down to me, Richard, and Gerald—the two other seniors who were trying out for the first time. Usually, if you didn't make varsity you were placed on junior varsity, which gave you a chance to play and practice more to get better for next season, rather than just sitting on the bench all the time. The JV had its own schedule of games, usually playing right before the varsity took the field. But this didn't apply to me, Richard, and Gerald since we were already twelfth graders and would be gone next year.

So after about a week of practice and with a decision to make, Coach Bob Branan had us three go through one final workout together to give him a chance for a concluding evaluation to see who'd get the single remaining uniform and coveted forest green Roughers jacket you got to wear at school, signifying you were an athlete.

He hit us grounders and watched us turn double plays with the starting shortstop, timed our speed around the bases, noting how we made the turn around first to second, and shot us fly balls in the outfield. They left the machine with a whomp, soaring tiny as a golf ball in the sky, and instead of arriving in a lazy direct bloop, curved like a boomerang. You had to sprint all out to a spot and adjust on the run. They were easy to overrun and the ball would drop behind you and roll to the fence. You'd look silly leaping into the air, scissoring your legs with your glove stabbing the air.

He had us throw from right field to third base, judging our

arms and checking to see if we hit our cutoff man. Gerald launched a throw that ballooned in the air for an eternity—allowing would-be runners to circle the bases—drawing laughter from some of the other players, and I knew he was cut right then.

Then Branan had us hit from the plate off the machine and we were about even in that competition. For a final appraisal he brought in a starting junior pitcher, Coleman "Dude" Hughes, and told him to throw us nothing but curveballs. Some say a curve is only an optical illusion, but they've never stood at home plate with the ball spinning at their head. It quits being an illusion if it hits you in the groin. Players bail out of the batter's box to avoid getting hit, then the ball dives over the plate and pops the catcher's mitt. Talk about looking silly.

Muskogee High School baseball coach and journalism teacher
Bob Branan. Branan was also a sportswriter who won an
Associated Press Sports Editors award for a series on Tommy
John ligament surgeries, written for the Muskogee Phoenix.
(Courtesy of Michael Branan.)

Upon Branan's instruction, Dude only threw us lazy curves, not the hard-biting sliders that zipped like the fastballs he was capable of. Richard and Gerald either whiffed every time or jumped out of the way. I timed them out, stood in instead of bailing, and rapped them into the outfield. The last one I bounced off the right field wall on one hop.

"Bring it in!" Branan yelled. He had everybody run laps around the outfield, telling us when we got back to the locker room the final roster would be posted on a sheet in the gym. I jogged around the warning track with Spencer, who was drafted by the Pittsburgh Pirates that June. He gathered with me, Richard, and Gerald in the gym and saw my name at the very bottom. I had made the team. Richard and Gerald didn't cry but looked like they wanted to, eyes shiny with disappointment and frowning faces. Now they had to hunt for a home-ec class or something else to fill up their last hour.

CHAPTER 31

COACH BRANAN GATHERED the team to talk about schedules for the semester. "You and you," he said at the end, pointing at me and Spencer, "will be in my first-hour journalism class."

Branan was a former *Phoenix* sportswriter and *Tulsa World* correspondent who ran the school paper and yearbook in addition to coaching baseball. Until then I had never given any thought to journalism or writing for the paper, although I sometimes wrote stories after the Dallas Cowboys lost that had them winning, with fake quotes from coach Tom Landry.

The first thing we learned in class were the five Ws—who, what, where, when, and why—that should be contained in the first paragraph of a story. Branan scribbled five facts on the chalkboard behind him and told us to write a "lede" paragraph including those items, keeping it to thirty-two words or less.

He gave us a few minutes and we passed our papers forward. At his desk, he read them quickly, stacking them in a pile. He withdrew one and read it aloud: "The Muskogee Board of Education on a 3–2 vote passed a resolution Thursday night allowing seniors to leave the school grounds for one hour at lunch, beginning next school year."

Bob Branan received a master's degree in journalism from the University of Oklahoma. I've always thought the Muskogee High School baseball field should be named in his honor. (Courtesy of Michael Branan.)

"Who wrote that?" he demanded, holding it in the air with a tight-lipped stare that I saw often on the baseball field. The way he said it, I thought I'd get in trouble if I raised my hand, but I did anyway.

"You get an A for the semester," he said.

We worked on ledes for almost the entire time I was in his class, it seemed.

"People, we are not moving on in this class until every single one of you can write a lead paragraph," he said in exasperation.

There was a photography darkroom behind the blackboard. You entered through a revolving circular door like a tall black can that kept light out. Sometimes he called his baseball players into the room and chewed them out for bad grades or absences. You'd hear his raised voice from the classroom.

I handed in a wrestling story for the *Scout*, the school newspaper, and was packing my bag at the end of class.

"Chuculate," Branan said, standing at the darkroom door. "Let me see you in here."

"Uh-oh," Spencer said under his breath.

Wondering what I'd done wrong on the story, I followed Branan in after the circular door revolved. He stood next to shallow trays of photo-developing liquid and machines that processed photos.

"The *Phoenix* needs help this football season," he said, his face bathed in the red darkroom light. "You'll be taking stats over the phone, writing stories on Friday nights for Saturday's paper."

He bent and scribbled on a notepad.

"Call Tommy Cummings at this number," he said, ripping the sheet off. "You start Friday."

With Branan it was never a question of if you wanted to do something, or any discussion of alternatives, it was just do it.

By the time I arrived, using a side-street entrance with a nondescript door rather than the front office, which was already closed at that hour, the newsroom was in full swing. Reporters sitting at desks clacked on keyboards with phones cradled to their ears amid a steady mix of chatter. Sports was filled in the rear, but someone usually found me an open desk toward the front in news. I always passed by a closed door that said JANITOR AND PUBLISHER, which intrigued me. I didn't ask about it at first since I had a million other things to learn.

The *Phoenix* covered about twenty-five high schools and three colleges in a seven-county area stretching to Arkansas. Tommy had an assistant sports editor and two full-time reporters and three or four regular stringers. With reporters at only four or five games, we were bombarded with phone calls from coaches or statisticians from about nine thirty to ten thirty anxious to get their games in Saturday morning's edition. You filled in sheets of paper with game statistics, including scoring by quarter, leading rushers, passers, defensive stars, who scored on what type of play and when, win-loss records, their next games, and got quotes from coaches.

With this information you filled out a prewritten box score on the computer—substituting XXs with actual numbers—and wrote five- or six-paragraph stories. It was tedious work at first, because in the rush you could forget to include essentials such as first names, grades, and where the game was played. Or you forgot to ask for it over the phone. Editors or reporters with sports backgrounds sometimes pitched in as did the staffers who had gone to games nearby and were back in the office. The education reporter and columnist Warren Weakland was a former longtime sports editor at the *Phoenix* and would take the occasional game story.

Phones rang continually this time of night and, anxious to help, I answered Weakland's phone while walking by and took another coach's call. He waited until I hung up and admonished me.

"Use your own phone next time, young man!" he said. To make matters worse I was sitting in his chair at his desk.

I noticed that Tommy plugged the stats right into the computer while on the phone instead of writing it on the sheet. He'd have the story almost written before he hung up with the coach. I began doing that, saving precious minutes as long as my info didn't disappear with a technical glitch. A wire editor helping me once punched a button that deleted my whole story. Unable to recover it I had to rewrite the whole thing in about ten minutes with the eleven-thirty deadline looming.

Every Saturday morning I clipped my stories into a scrapbook. My name didn't appear with these articles—that was reserved for when you actually went to the contests. I was doing well at writing the summaries from the phone so Tommy began sending me to games.

This was no less hectic, because after they were over I compiled the stats myself, interviewed coaches and players on the field or in the locker room, and drove back to the paper mentally framing the story, and then wrote it in under an hour. The shirt sticking to my back and the cool air on my skin when I left the newsroom alerted me I'd been sweating.

My first byline appeared early the next year from a Muskogee wrestling match at the MHS gym. Anxious to finally see my name above an article for the first time, I was horrified to open the paper in the morning and see "By Ed Chuculate/Phoenix Special Writer."

Ed, I thought, made me sound like my grandpa instead of the seventeen years old I had turned since I started at the *Phoenix*. No one called me Ed, so I requested the somewhat ostentatious "Eddie Del Chuculate" as if my middle name distinguished me from the throngs of Eddie Chuculates already in existence. With "Del," I was acknowledging Homer—Delbert Ezell "Homer" Flanary.

By this time, I was growing more comfortable in the newsroom. I'd grab a handful of M&Ms out of the bowl on the city desk and look at the day's edition the head editor tacked on a corkboard after going through it with his red pen. He had underlined a small stretch of gibberish like "#%&!@" that appeared in the middle of a sentence and wrote "RAILROADING COPY!" above it. I asked Coach Branan what that meant, and he said they had published the story without editing it, probably running late against deadline.

Around midnight you'd hear the presses in back begin to run. I finally asked about the mysterious "Janitor and Publisher" office, because with my night hours I saw neither a janitor nor a publisher around.

One of the reporters told me that a new publisher—a person

who pretty much owns the whole paper—was looking for something in the custodian's supply area. The longtime janitor walked in and found him snooping around.

"What are you doing here? This is the janitor's closet. It's my room!"

"I'm the publisher. I own this place and I can be here if I want to."

The janitor retaliated: "It doesn't say publisher on the door, it says janitor."

The next day the publisher had a new sign engraved: JANITOR AND PUBLISHER.

As the season wore on and my bylines accumulated, Tommy began assigning me college football. I'd cover a high school game in neighboring Gore, population 900, on Friday night, and be at an Oklahoma State University game in Stillwater the next afternoon with 50,000 in attendance.

It was fun at first seeing my stories being read by classmates or teachers at school with my byline at the top or taking friends to the school library to see my articles. But it wasn't so much fun when I had to put my teammates' names in stories when they made a costly error or struck out in a crucial situation; yet I had to. I was confronted a few times in the locker room over this. But I also included them when they hit a home run, struck out twelve batters, or made a deep throw from shortstop to end an inning.

Before I started covering games, though, I had to get my driver's license. Through my friend Dana, I met her uncle, Johnny Tiger, Jr., who sometimes dropped me off at the newsroom and picked me up around midnight until he took me for my road test. He was an internationally known artist everyone called "Uncle," and had been raised with my uncles at the West Eufaula Indian Baptist Church campgrounds. It wasn't until later I realized he was the same dazzling "Tony Tiger" I'd met with Granny at Safeway when I was in grade school.

I had limited experience on the road, mainly in driver's ed in Milburn and Muskogee, where we sat behind the wheel in arcade-like simulators and drove along with a film shown on a screen at the front of the room. I had studied the booklet and already passed the written exam. I drove to the DMV in Uncle's sleek white 1980 Corvette, which he pinstriped himself in thin red strips along the sides and over the fenders. This was the only time I'd driven it but he thought the ten miles from his house in Gooseneck Bend to the bureau should be enough.

The Oklahoma Highway Patrol trooper administering my driving test knocked off his tall gold-tasseled Smokey Bear hat climbing into the car. I say climbing in, but in a car that hugs the ground like that it's more like dropping into a cockpit: It's as if you're sitting on the road. That flustered the trooper—he already looked in a bad mood—and when he tried to put the hat back on it mashed against the roof and wouldn't fit so he held it in his lap.

He directed me north along East Side Boulevard. Taking off from the first light I mashed too hard on the gas and the acceleration snapped his head back. He didn't necessarily think this was funny. The ride was jarring on rough city streets but smooth on Shawnee Bypass as we passed Bacone College and Muskogee High and turned onto the Muskogee Turnpike. The car responded to the slightest pressure on the pedal and in trying to feather it just right my speed fluctuated. I may have eclipsed the 55 mph limit.

We exited the turnpike and at the intersection of Callahan and East Side Boulevard next to Lakeland Shopping Center just a few blocks from the DMV I stopped at a red light. There was no painted crosswalk, but the trooper later said I had crossed it—possible since the Corvette had such a long nose it was difficult to gauge.

Waiting outside in the car, Uncle thought I was joking when I said I'd failed but laughed when I told him about snapping the trooper's head back.

"No wonder he flunked you," he said.

We tried again a few days later in his Chevy Cheyenne pickup, his regular day-to-day driver, but no less spiffy: metallic blue and silver with tinted windows, shiny chrome wheels, a black snap-on tarp over the bed, Bose system, and plenty of headroom to fit an Oklahoma trooper wearing a Smokey Bear hat.

I had driven this truck many more times than the Corvette, had a different trooper, and drove nearly the same route without any problems. Thirty minutes later, I was a licensed driver. I didn't know who was happier, Uncle or myself.

CHAPTER 32

DURING PRACTICE, BRANAN called me off the field.

"Chuculate! Come here!" he said, cupping his hands around his mouth and waving me to the dugout. "Someone needs to talk to you!"

I jogged over. He was standing next to a man in glasses carrying a clipboard and wearing a green Northeastern (OK) State University windbreaker.

"Ooh, Chook getting recruited!" Clyde yelled from center field.

Toward the end of the season, you'd see scouts wearing their college gear in the stands, holding radar guns—mainly for Spencer— and chatting to players after games.

I didn't even start and only played a few times, pinch-hitting or running or defense in late innings. Branan had already told me this before the season opener—due to my late arrival to the program as a senior, and barely making the team anyway—when he saw me disgruntled and sulking at the end of the bench with other players, our hands stuffed into our crotches to keep our fingers warm during an early March game.

He came over and pointed at me.

"I told you we'd use you when we need you!" he barked. End of discussion.

So, how was it I was being recruited?

The man said he was the sports information director (SID) at NSU, a state school about thirty miles away in Tahlequah, and Branan had told him about how I was writing sports for the *Muskogee Phoenix*. The SID, also a former *Phoenix* sports editor, said there was funding and work-study aid available if I would consider enrolling at NSU in the fall. The position entailed writing press releases on practices and games and feature stories for NSU athletics and keeping statistics. Branan had realized my future didn't contain playing baseball but writing about it.

I had planned on going to college but there was no painstaking selection process or multiple applications or fingernail chewing over acceptance letters coming in the mail. Momma only went a semester at Oklahoma State Tech in Okmulgee when I was four, and Shorty lasted a day after taking a train to Haskell vocational school for Indian students in Lawrence, Kansas, after high school, so there was no grand family legacy to uphold. Being on the baseball team and school paper, it seemed everyone around me was going to college and it was a natural next step for me as well. Spencer even turned down the Pirates to go to baseball powerhouse Connors State College in nearby Warner. He was drafted higher by the Texas Rangers a few years later. My friend Darrin Walters was heading off to OU.

Due to my status as a Native American and my above-average ACT scores, I had received letters of interest from most Big Eight Conference schools, including OU and Oklahoma State, and even Dartmouth. Dartmouth: I pronounced it "Dart-MOUTH" and couldn't even find it on a map. Since I had an offer from NSU with a financial-aid package laid out that included journalism and sports, and it was just down the highway, I enrolled there in the fall. Being nearby, I could continue stringing for the *Phoenix*. But the work-study writing job included lugging twenty-pound pop canisters up thirty flights of stairs to the press box at the football stadium. Hindsight is twenty-twenty, but I should have looked into Dartmouth a little harder.

CHAPTER 33

I'D KNOWN DARRIN since my one-day stint at Harris-Jobe in sixth grade and also at Sadler, but we didn't start hanging out much together until I bumped into him while roaming the Muskogee Public Library shelves when we were in high school. He lived nearby and I'd go to his place on South 7th and listen to records: Run-DMC, Kurtis Blow, Whodini, Van Halen. I'd spend the night and we'd get up in the morning to play tennis at Spaulding Park before it got too hot, then return in the evening after it cooled off.

Before graduation, Darrin's mom, Shirley, wanted us to ride to the 7-Eleven on Broadway and 9th with her. When we pulled up there was a group of teens standing around the payphones in front of the store, joking around and being loud. Shirley dug in her purse for money, glancing up at the group, but never got out. People went in and out, paying for gas or leaving with drinks and bags of items. Other groups stood outside their cars with stereos blasting, talking and visiting. We just sat there staring at the store.

"Would you two go in and get me a pack of menthols?" she asked, holding some bills and change. This was when you could buy cigarettes at age sixteen.

We got out.

Darrin Walters (left) and me, both nineteen, in July 1986, just outside Austin, Texas, for Farm Aid. Using my media credentials, I wrangled two backstage passes. The shirt I'm wearing was designed by Johnny Tiger "Uncle" Jr. Willie Nelson signed this shirt for me on the moon in upper left while I was wearing it. Ironically, he knew Tiger and had previously purchased some of his artwork. (Courtesy of the author.)

"Hey, there go Chuculate!"

It was my old Pershing teammate Tony Tollett over by the phones holding a Big Gulp and bag of Cheetos. Tollett had borrowed a jacket from me that semester and wore it for a week, returning it with hair grease on the collar because he always strutted around wearing it flipped up. He'd once said to me at school, staring down at my feet, "Chook be puttin' some *wear* on some shoes."

I said hey to everyone, executing the handshake we all did involving a circuit of snapping, clapping, and pointing, and went into the store. It was packed with customers as we roamed the aisles for snacks.

"Damn," Darrin said, "we're the only white people in here."

I looked at him incredulously. "I'm not white!" I shot back.

The group around the phones yelled and pointed at me again when I came out.

Shirley put the car in reverse. "Eddie, you know everybody around here, don't you?" she said.

Throughout my school years, I heard people say, "I'm part Indian but I don't claim it." I never knew if it was derogatory or they were parroting their parents. How times have changed: Anyone with a sixteenth claims it now. By the time our senior class had started first grade, Muskogee schools had been integrated for two years and the races grew up together not knowing they'd once been separated. Most prejudice was shown in class distinction: rich or poor.

I definitely fell into the latter camp. I felt more ostracized for not wearing the right jeans or qualifying for free lunch than for the color of my skin. Talk of vacations at Yellowstone or summer camps was completely foreign to me as was what kind of car I was getting when I got my license. We were lucky just to keep a vehicle running at home and I always took the bus or got rides.

I never had money for Polo or Izod shirts or name-brand sporting gear, so to try and fit in I made my own. Homer had a plain blue-green cloth jacket hanging in a closet that he never wore. It was too big for me, but I took it down and super-glued an Izod alligator off an old shirt I found somewhere and wore it to school a few days before the alligator fell off and I tossed the jacket in my locker.

I took my $10 Kmart tennis racket I played with at Spaulding and converted it into a $200 Prince version by stenciling a big angular *P* on the strings with a felt marker. It left black marks on the balls and faded after a few weeks until I was left with the generic model again. It didn't matter anyway because my game didn't improve using the Prince knockoff.

I spent most of high school living under self-conscious clouds of poverty and low self-esteem after being expelled in Tishomingo. But I was soaked with sunrays of confidence when I began writing for the paper. Even if I didn't have a car, wear high-dollar clothes, or eat lunch at the country club, seeing my name on the page sprouted an inner identity to replace poor boy, sneak-thief, and vandal.

I could have landed in an institutional trap, a chain of detention centers, if I had been jailed for destroying the band room. My influences would have been inmates instead of coaches and editors. And although the checks I received for writing articles weren't large, cashing them was huge as I was using my mind to finally earn my own money. They became bonuses as it didn't even feel like work.

Money affords the wealthy time to cultivate their talents, but not all the wealthy are talented and not all take advantage of it. Most have to recognize the opportunity when it arises, seize it, and find time for their passion while working to pay rent and keep food in the refrigerator. If some people are born on third base and spend their whole life thinking they hit a triple, the rest of us have to beat out bunts, steal second, and dive into third on a sacrifice fly. After dusting yourself off, at least you know you worked hard to arrive, and scoring from there tastes even sweeter.

One occasion from high school sticks out, however. We gathered at a party one Saturday night at a kid's house whose parents were gone. Couples began pairing up and I found myself with a blond-haired white girl. We had our arms around each other's shoulders, sitting on a couch with other couples listening to music. I can't even remember her name or if I ever saw her again. She was on the end against an armrest and Stewart McKenzie, a white boy I knew and had ridden around with a few times, leaned down to her and said, "What are you doing with this Indian kid when you could be with me?"

He wasn't trying to whisper or necessarily be loud about it. He said it like I wasn't even there, never acknowledging me, but I heard it plainly, and so did the girl as he said it right in her ear. I waited for some response from her, as did McKenzie, like "mind your own business" or "buzz off" or something, but we resumed talking like *he* wasn't even there and he walked away. I guess I didn't need to say anything. I was the one with my arm around her.

That was an isolated incident for me growing up. There were usually so many other people like me around that I always felt comfortable in Muskogee, unlike some other towns. McKenzie's comment didn't floor me—I've never even told anyone until now—because I knew he wasn't representative of all whites, and as a person I couldn't care less what he thought. But it has made me think about where he got his attitude and how many more people walk around with it.

I WENT ON to collect 226 bylines for the *Muskogee Phoenix*. I covered my beloved Dallas Cowboys, bypassing miles of bumper-to-bumper highway game traffic on a dedicated lane with my press pass, parking right next to the stadium, and walking through a tunnel onto the field I had previously seen only on TV. I ate next to the famous broadcaster Pat Summerall at halftime and interviewed players in the locker room after the game, snatching a pair of Cowboys wristbands—white with a blue star—still in their package off the carpeted floor. Wearing them playing basketball a few weeks later, I was asked where I got them and was not believed when I said the Dallas locker room.

Writing down lineups at the scorer's table before the start of a basketball game in Warner, I looked up to see my first baseball coach, A. C. Richardson, who'd awarded me the MVP aluminum bat when I was six that I dragged to school every day. He also taught at MHS and I'd see him occasionally at games.

Dressed in his referee's uniform, he was checking in with the official scorer and timer when he saw me.

"Hey, Chook!" he said, spinning the ball in his hands. "You writing this for the *Phoenix*?"

"Yep," I said. "You're still reffing, obviously."

He took the whistle out of his mouth while backpedaling to center court to jump the ball. "Beats pullin' cotton, don't it?"

I saw Coach Branan in the press box when we were both covering a Sooners game for the *Phoenix* in Manhattan, Kansas. I told him how a friend and I drove state highways instead of the interstate and got lost during the night, arriving in the morning and getting caught in the homecoming parade. I thought he'd find it funny.

"That was stupid," he said in his typical no-nonsense style. By then, though, I was accustomed to it.

Instead of using a laptop the *Phoenix* issued him that he was unfamiliar with, he dictated his story over the phone back to the newsroom. When I read his long article the next morning in the paper, I was amazed he was able to write it without sitting and typing, instead standing and flipping through his notes, rattling off the whole story into the phone off the top of his head, quotes and all. I wrote mine on a laptop from a Pizza Hut in Manhattan.

Covering the annual OU-Texas rivalry at the Cotton Bowl in Dallas, I wandered up the tunnel prior to kickoff as the Sooners emptied out of their locker room, and I managed to glimpse legendary Coach Barry Switzer dwarfed among the players. I stopped to admire the capacity crowd of seventy-five thousand or so—half wearing red, the other half orange, against a crystal-blue October sky. Suddenly I heard a hundred pairs of stampeding cleats as the team ran down the ramp. I had no choice but to run, too, and later Momma, who was watching astounded on national television, said it looked like I was leading Switzer, the players, and banner-waving cheerleaders onto the field.

At the *Okmulgee Daily Times*, I won first place in the state of Oklahoma for sports columns. Other newspaper jobs took me elsewhere, including Tulsa, Fort Worth, Albuquerque, Denver, Minneapolis, and even Abu Dhabi in the United Arab Emirates. I also wrote personal columns and magazine articles and began writing fiction, winning a two-year creative writing fellowship at Stanford University.

Walking to the Green Library one day, I was passed by two girls who laid their bikes down and bounced up the stairs in front of me. I looked up to see then-US president Bill Clinton's daughter, Chelsea, also a student there, holding the door open for me.

I later won an O. Henry Award, the oldest major literary prize in America for short fiction, and published a book of short stories, *Cheyenne Madonna*, with Black Sparrow Press in Boston.

It wouldn't have happened without Coach Branan's intervention in my life, which is why sports and other extracurricular activities are important even if they don't lead to a pro career. Without telling me, Branan contacted a college recruiter on my behalf. He didn't have to do that. He also cared enough to refer me to the *Phoenix*, for which I've been forever grateful as it led to a life of writing. He didn't have to do that, either. I'm also glad he didn't cut me from the Roughers because I never would have taken his journalism class, which led to everything else. Could it all be because I hit Dude's last curve to the outfield wall?

I went back to Muskogee recently and spent a night at Lonnie's. He let me sleep in his bed and he took the couch. The next day he wanted to eat some catfish he caught at Lock and Dam 17, a spot on the Verdigris River north of town where I had first fished with Homer when I was a kid. It was too hot to cook in the kitchen, so Lonnie built a small fire outside in a ring of rocks. When it settled, he put a grate over the rocks and brought out a skillet. It was breezy under the shade trees and his beagles frolicked around his pickup with their droopy ears flopping, thinking we were going somewhere.

After the grease started bubbling, he dropped in the cornmeal-coated nuggets, his hands speckled with flour. He wore a white tank top, and I saw he still had the scar from the fiddleback bite. He flipped the pieces around with a fork and when they floated and were golden brown, he took them out and put them on paper plates.

We ate with our fingers, sitting on his tailgate. Fishing poles, rakes, and shovels lined the bed of the truck. He tossed a piece of fish to one of the beagles, who snatched it from the air. The other began to bark and howl, mournful sounds that sent remembrances swimming over me: hunting and fishing, Granny and Homer, freezing winter mornings, country roads, my great-uncle Chester.

Even though Lonnie and I rarely if ever talked about the day Chester snatched him by the throat and cussed him, I can't help but think about it every time I see him, and fill with regret. I wonder now how I would have felt or reacted if it had happened to me: if Lonnie's uncle had grabbed me by the neck when I was at his house and slurred me in my face, how scared I would have been. Sometimes when I hear that word, I picture Lonnie's frightened face, his terrified eyes, and it stops me cold.

"C'moan, Chook," Lonnie said, finishing his fish and throwing the plate into a barrel where he burned trash. "Let's take a ride."

The beagles jumped onto the tailgate and into the back and we drove along 24th Street across Shawnee to Harris Road. On Harris he turned east. I thought we were taking the dogs down to the river, but he turned onto 17th and past the Ledbetter place I saw the little house on the hill through the trees.

"I thought you might want to see your old house," he said. "Every time I go by, I'm surprised it's still standing. Next time you come back it probably won't even be here."

It was overgrown with weeds and a portion of the roof had caved in, taking the red chimney with it. We parked at the gate and I stretched the barbed-wire fence so Lonnie could dip through and he did the same for me. The dogs scampered ahead through the pasture, which had reclaimed the garden and even the yard around the house.

But the oak tree where I shot at birds was still there in the corner, growing larger as we neared. A swarm of sparrows arrived in a dark wedge, swooped over it in formation like a spinning wheel, then all landed, disappearing into the canopy of leaves like magic. It struck me that I no longer shot at birds, but fed them instead. I began to wonder how I could have spent so much time alone out here growing up, having two sisters and a brother. I realized I never had the chance to be the big brother I could have been, moving around so much. The few times we all lived together, I took it for granted, thinking it would be forever.

At the house, the front porch had rotted so we stepped in gingerly. It seemed incredibly tiny, just four small doorless rooms forming a square with the little bathroom on the side. Dust swirled in shafts of light from holes in the ceiling like snow in a paperweight. The kitchen cabinets Homer built were still in good condition, however, like they could have been made yesterday. There was a Kerr's jar of Granny's bacon grease in one of them, still sealed.

We stepped into the living room. The stove in the corner where we huddled for warmth was gone, but marks on the cracked linoleum indicated where it stood under a spot on the ceiling blackened from soot. In the bathroom cabinet I found one of Homer's old steel Gillette razors. I turned the handle and the jaws opened. I put it in my pocket.

In their closet above a dusty box of Granny's *Organic Gardening* magazines dated 1977 a forgotten blue sweater hung on a lone hanger. In one of the deep pockets I found pink tissue paper, still soft. I took that as well. I brought a sleeve of the sweater to my nose, inhaled the smell, and exhaled memories: I was always hot in here in the summer and could see my breath on December mornings; the floors were hard and cold with no carpet; I couldn't call anyone because we didn't have a phone; I couldn't watch color cable TV; I had to walk a mile to go to the store. It was the best time of my life.

I was at first angered at the condition of the old place, then saddened, then relieved that Lonnie had brought me. I understood just how spartan my existence had been, but also overflowing with fresh food, books, exercise, love, and happiness.

Outside, Lonnie whistled for his dogs—a long, looping shrill with his fingers against his lips that ended on a piercing high note. I joined him out front and we scanned east across the fields where the KMUS radio towers blinked in the chalk-blue sky, but we didn't see the dogs. Only a lone quail answered. As Lonnie raised his hand to whistle again, a rabbit darted from the old garden and stopped, ears flat. Almost immediately the dogs splashed through the tangled weeds, barking and howling. The rabbit reached the fence in three bounding leaps with the dogs chasing, and they vanished except for a current of movement snaking through the tall grass.

Lonnie laughed. "There they go again," he said.

We walked after them. Lonnie stood on the bottom strand of barbed wire and lifted the middle to let me duck under, and I did the same for him.

Q&A WITH EDDIE CHUCULATE

Q: Eddie, what inspired you to write your memoir?

A: There are so many aspects to Native American life: coastal tribes, reservations on the Plains, inland California, communities in the Southeast mountains, pueblos in the Southwest, Great Lakes nations, Pacific Northwest, nations in Minnesota and New York, but I hadn't read much of growing up in what I'd consider Middle America. About Native youth who joined Cub Scouts, played little league baseball, or fed quarters to video games at the grocery store.

Q: What do you hope readers will take away from reading this book?

A: That such life experiences as I've described do exist, but that no matter where or how you're raised, you'll be confronted with universal problems—racism, poverty, bullying, temptation—and you can and should make your own decisions and set your own course. To look at people for what's inside them rather than outward appearances. That rebellion and challenging the status quo can be beneficial, but respect for authority is also a must.

Q: Many stories by or about Native Americans encompass some element of trauma, but as you noted once, your story does not come from a place of trauma. How do you wish for this book to contribute to the story of the modern Native American experience?

A: Since we were here first, all the problems that you see or read about in media and popular culture associated with Native Americans were introduced or created by other races—dumped on us. It's taking forever, but we're slowly evolving away from this. Natives are becoming known for grander things. We're both members of modern American society *and* of a particular tribe or tribes—exclusive clubs stretching coast-to-coast where you can also be admitted as members.

Q: What themes of your story do you think will most resonate with contemporary young adult readers?

A: You can create or change your own identity and not follow the herd. And the power of love—between children and parents, between friends, between sisters and brothers—is undeniable.

Q: How does the theme of second chances play into your own personal history?

A: I've been given second chances to continue jobs, continue school, continue educational programs, and, as a result, continue writing. When you realize you've been given second chances and have taken advantage of them, you're more likely to give deserved second chances as well.

Q: Is there anything else you would like to share with readers?

A: Any particular book by a Native American shouldn't be viewed as representative of the entire race. As I've mentioned, the life experience is greatly varied, as are the authors and their genres.

ACKNOWLEDGMENTS

My agent, Alex Glass, of Glass Literary Management, continues to believe in me and was the genesis for this book. He's a wellspring of inspiration, confidence, and guidance.

Lisa Ann Sandell, my editor at Scholastic, posed insightful questions, forced me to confront difficult situations, and provided invaluable direction.

The poet Jon Davis at the Institute of American Indian Arts encouraged me to pursue creative writing and stood with me in troubling times.

To my Bezzell cousins, Gloria, Twilley, Ashlee Clark, Emmanuel, and Greg (my little homie named Malik), you are my truly loving family.

To Twin Cities friends Adam Krause, Lisa Legge, Kaira Williams, and Rachelle Hawkins: Thanks for your support and encouragement. Dr. Ann Ong in Muskogee threw a lifeline, and Darrin J. Walters in Norman, Oklahoma, was a fountain of knowledge and insight. Mike Kays and Melony Carey in Muskogee, and George Flanary in Wagoner, Oklahoma, were helpful as well.

Melissa "Missy" Green, Brittney Ann Bezzell, Clifton Cayaditto, and Della Ruth (Youngbear) French: Are there really no more tears in heaven?

My cousin Russell Newman provided some family background, and Michael Branan, Melita Griffith, and David Barnett supplied family photographs. Barnett also verified information concerning his uncle, the Rev. Austin Barnett, and his father, Edmond Barnett, Jr. Thank you for your cooperation.

Former *Muskogee Daily Phoenix* coworker Betty (Smith) Ridge's memoir, *Deadlines*, is a firsthand account of newsroom culture for women in the 1970s and 1980s and supplied some *Phoenix* background.

For Muscogee (Creek) words not spelled phonetically, I consulted *Dictionary Muskokee and English*, by Rev. R. M. Loughridge and David M. Hodge, and *A Dictionary of Creek/Muskogee*, by Jack B. Martin and Margaret McKane Mauldin.

ABOUT THE AUTHOR

Eddie Chuculate is Creek and Cherokee Indian and originally from Muskogee, Oklahoma. Writing that he began at the Institute of American Indian Arts in Santa Fe, New Mexico, won him a Wallace Stegner Creative Writing Fellowship at Stanford University in Palo Alto, California. The first story from his collection *Cheyenne Madonna* (Black Sparrow Press, Boston) won a PEN/O. Henry Prize and was selected by juror Ursula K. Le Guin as her favorite of that year. After that publication, he earned a master's degree at the University of Iowa Writers' Workshop. Chuculate began a journalism career at age sixteen, while still in high school in Muskogee, and he went on to write and edit for several metro daily newspapers. He has also picked pecans, moved furniture, worked as a day laborer, received food stamps, and sold his plasma in five states. Eddie has lived in Hanna, Oklahoma; Jemez Pueblo, New Mexico; Abu Dhabi, United Arab Emirates; Portland, Maine; Albuquerque; San Francisco; Oakland; and Denver; and he now resides in downtown Minneapolis.